NEW KEY GEOGRAPHY

Foundations
Teacher's Resource

COLETTE ASHBY
DAVID COOKSON
GRANT WESTOBY

Nelson Thornes

Published in 2006 by:
Nelson Thornes Ltd
Delta Place
27 Bath Road
CHELTENHAM
GL53 7TH
United Kingdom

12 / 10 9

A catalogue record for this book is available from the British Library

ISBN 978-07487-9704-2

Illustrations by Gordon Lawson, Angela Lumley, Richard Morris,
David Russell Illustration

Page make-up by Viners Wood Associates

Printed and bound in Great Britain by Berforts Group

Acknowledgements

With thanks to the following for permission to reproduce photographs and other copyright
material in this book:

Cover photos: Waterfall, Loch Awe, Scotland by Joe Cornish/ Digital Vision LL (NT) (left);
Jakarta, Indonesian floods by Crack/ Reuters/ Corbis (centre); Foster building ('Gherkin'),
London by John Begg Photography/ Photographers Direct (right).

Connors/ Nigel Bowles: 77; Corbis/ Reuters/ Rafiqur Rahman: 86; Digital Vision 15 (NT):
87; Eye Ubiquitous: 81 (top and middle); Foster building ('Gherkin'), London by John Begg
Photography/ Photographers Direct: 33; Caroline Malatesta/ Birmingham News, Alabama:
137; York and County Press: 81 (bottom).

Extract on page 124 from *Gridlock* by Ben Elton © Time Warner Book Group UK, 1991, and
reproduced with kind permission.

Every effort has been made to contact copyright holders and we apologise if any have been
overlooked.

Contents

Teacher's Resource CD-ROM

The accompanying CD-ROM provides you with:

- All activity sheets from the Teacher's Resource, in convenient PDF format
- Editable activity sheets for each unit
- Unit Plans and Schemes of Work – ready to use or customisable
- Useful activity 'masters' to support pupil book activities

NEW KEY GEOGRAPHY Series Overview

Teacher's Resources

- Activity sheets for every topic
- Resources and support for implementing Assessment for Learning throughout each topic
- Opportunities to develop geographical and thinking skills
- Integral CD-ROM with editable activities, customisable lesson planning support and additional resources.

Teacher's Handbooks

- Use with the Pupil Books and Teacher's Resources to provide at-a-glance lesson support
- Includes easy-to-follow overviews, starter and plenary ideas, homework suggestions, answers to the activities and more – for every topic.

New Key Geography Pupil Books

- Core resources and activities for all ability levels
- Introductory spreads to stimulate interest in each topic
- Offers clear progression through each topic
- Highly visual with striking photographs to help engage pupils.

Kerboodle Online Books

- Online versions of the Pupil Books that can be accessed in school or at home
- Provides 24/7 access to the book for all your students
- Easy-to-use toolset allows you to personalise the textbook by adding notes, highlights, pen annotations and weblinks
- Pupils can view your personalised copy of the book online and add their own annotations to their individual copies to help with revision and independent learning.

Basics

- One-volume supplementary resource for further differentiation
- Resources and activities to be used alongside the core texts
- Helps to improve performance and increase confidence
- Encourages progression in skills, knowledge and understanding.

Introduction to the

NEW KEY GEOGRAPHY

Foundations Teacher's Resource

While the *New Key Geography Foundations* pupil book has been revised and updated to include new material, new topics and new features, the *New Key Geography Foundations* Teacher's Resource is completely new. All the activity sheets are new, and particular attention has been given to age-appropriate tasks that develop and further extend each double-page spread in the pupil book. Some of the activity sheets may be seen as templates that teachers could develop and use as patterns for developing their own activities and enquiries. Indeed, many of the activity sheets are also provided in an editable format on the accompanying CD-ROM, allowing teachers to customise the activities for their own pupils. In addition, a new Scheme of Work is provided for each unit. These are modelled on the familiar format of the QCA Schemes of Work and can be adapted easily to meet the requirements of individual departments.

There is also support for implementing key elements of the KS3 National Strategy, in particular Assessment for Learning, lesson planning, thinking skills and ICT. The importance now given to Assessment for Learning in the classroom is acknowledged with the provision of integrated assessment for learning activities, pupils' self-assessment resources, and supporting notes for the teacher.

Unlike many other teacher resources, there are no answers here. Each photocopiable activity encourages active participation rather than rote learning, and serves to reward the process rather than simply emphasising a correct answer. Importantly, the Teacher's Resource provides evaluative measures from individual exercises and involves pupils in their own learning. An expectation of these resources is that they will easily fit into individual departments' Schemes of Work. It is not anticipated that the teacher will necessarily use every activity, but rather will select those tasks that best suit and consolidate their pupils' learning needs.

However, the previous *Key Geography New Foundations* Teacher's Resource Guide (ISBN 0 7487 6073 3) has not been made redundant – the new Teacher's Resource should be seen as a natural extension and up-to-date addition to the previous publication. Importantly, almost all of the activity sheets and most of the assessments from the previous Teacher's Resource Guide can still be used.

The range of resources offered by *Key Geography* continues to grow and widen, allowing teachers increasing scope to develop courses adapted to meet the demands and needs both of their teaching and their pupils' learning. The material also has a content and style that allows it to be purposefully used with mixed-ability teaching groups and which relates to other KS3 programmes of study available to secondary schools.

Curriculum planning

The QCA Scheme of Work provides the obvious model for curriculum planning in secondary school departments. A blank copy of the geography outline can be downloaded from the DfEE Standards website at www.standards.dfee.gov.uk/.

The Schemes of Work have been completely revised and updated for *New Key Geography Foundations*. Each Scheme of Work starts with a general introduction to each unit before going on to describe each lesson or group of lessons in more detail.

The Schemes of Work contain the following elements:

About the unit
This section provides space to outline the general features of the unit of work and gives an estimate of the length of teaching time needed. This should give departmental staff, supply teachers, school management, inspectors and other parties who have a legitimate interest, a general idea of the main thrust of the unit of work.

Key aspects
This section should include, where relevant, the following:

- ◆ Geographical enquiry skills.
- ◆ Knowledge and understanding of places.
- ◆ Knowledge and understanding of patterns and processes.
- ◆ Knowledge and understanding of environmental change and sustainable development.

Expectations

This section provides space to say what pupils are expected to gain from the unit. It is divided into three subsections:

1 At the end of this unit most pupils will...
2 At the end of this unit some pupils will not have made so much progress and will...
3 At the end of this unit some pupils will have progressed further and will...

These subsections should combine statements from the descriptors of levels of attainment with statements about the opportunities for reaching those levels, which are provided by the content of the unit in question.

Prior learning

Where possible, statements in this section should link the work being done in the unit to work that has been done in previous years of the pupils' geography course and in primary school.

Language for learning

This section might contain references to specialist vocabulary that should be used and learned, and also highlight opportunities that pupils might be given to use language skills in reading, writing, listening and speaking. This, in turn, can make a modest contribution towards addressing and enhancing the role of reading in the secondary school geography curriculum. Cross-references to the whole-school programme for language development might be included here too.

Resources

Here, departments might list the resources that are available and which might be used to supplement *New Key Geography Foundations*. Reference might also be made to the *New Key Geography Foundations* Teacher's Resource; *New Key Geography Connections*; *New Key Geography Interactions*; *Key Geography New Places*; *Basics* and *Extensions*; the *Key Geography* website; OS maps; atlases; ICT-based resources (the internet); whiteboard activities such as the *New Key Geography Foundations Electronic Resources*; and to the teacher's own printed and electronic resources developed for use with *Key Geography*.

Future learning

Reference may be made to other units in *New Key Geography* that are directly dependent on the mastery of this unit, or to those that might allow pupils to fill the gaps left by the unit. In later units, reference might be made to preparation for courses leading to external examinations.

Links

Links to other subjects and cross-curricular skills can be made here, as well as to key skills, geographical skills and thinking skills. It might be particularly valuable to refer to citizenship and ICT. When schools are carrying out audits of their provision in these areas, it is important that geography departments can point out the many references to these topics that are already in their Schemes of Work.

Lesson plans

These lesson plans have been completely revised and updated for *New Key Geography Foundations*. The plans directly link objectives to outcomes and list possible resources and learning activities. There are detailed references to the content of the new editions of the pupil books and the activities in the new Teacher's Resource. There are also references to *Key Geography* supplementary resources – *Key Geography New Places*, *Basics*, *Extensions* and *Skills*, and to the Nelson Thornes website. However, these are not exhaustive and departments will want to find other ways of extending their teaching of the pupil book topics than those mentioned here.

Suggestions are made in the Schemes of Work that are not supported by *Key Geography* resources. There are many possible extension activities that move teachers and pupils on from the pupil books. All departments will surely be on the lookout for such extensions that suit the needs and circumstances of their pupils and their departments. The further development of resources for pupils of all abilities, and indeed for the needs of each individual pupil, is likely to become a central issue in curriculum planning. The Schemes of Work provided on the CD-ROM are simply a convenient starting point for the department's own development of ideas and resources.

Unit Overviews

These are provided to help teachers to see 'at a glance' what each unit contains and how it might be used. These include a summary of the key questions for the unit and of the skills and vocabulary that will be needed, with links to the Programme of Study and the content of the pupil book.

ICT in *New Key Geography Foundations*

At KS3 there are statutory requirements to use ICT. The *New Key Geography* resources provide opportunities for using ICT throughout. The Schemes of Work provided for each unit identify ICT opportunities for individual topics. The Teacher's Resource activities also provide ICT opportunities linked to the units in the pupil book. The activities in the Teacher's Resource are also supplied on the accompanying CD-ROM. Many of these are also provided in an editable format to be customised and adapted by the teacher to meet the needs of their own pupils, and can also be completed on-screen by the pupils themselves.

New Key Geography offers a wide range of new multi-media electronic resources, linked to the content of each spread in the pupil books, to develop pupils' ICT capability and enhance the quality of their learning experience in geography.

Ideas for integrating ICT with *New Key Geography Foundations* are available on the *Key Geography* website. As well as providing links to other relevant sites, the *New Key Geography Foundations* site includes a collection of web enquiries, which link to the activities provided in the *New Key Geography Foundations* pupil book.

The *Key Geography* website: http://www.nelsonthornes.com/secondary/geography/index.htm

From the Homepage, go to 'KS3 Links' to access the *New Key Geography Foundations* resources.

Teaching and learning with *New Key Geography Foundations*

At a time of curriculum change, geography teachers are being given more and more responsibility for devising the learning materials which are needed to respond to new syllabuses, new teaching methods and new modes of assessment. The National Curriculum now demands that all subjects at KS3 include 'teaching thinking'. Furthermore, 'thinking and learning skills' is highlighted within the 'Strategy for the Foundation Subjects at KS3' document and is increasingly being promoted across the age and ability range. Its rationale is simple: to raise standards in geography with the aim of making it a more challenging subject that focuses on helping KS3 pupils become better learners.

Thinking and learning

For some time now teachers and educationalists have encouraged the view that 'thinking and learning' skills are needed across all the subjects and the refinement of these skills should be actively fostered across the age and ability range. The *New Key Geography Foundations* Teacher's Resource focuses on the promotion of thinking through geography and has been written with one overriding purpose in mind: to show what pupils know, understand and can do. It advocates collaborative working and learning through communication and further contributes to the National Curriculum's Key Skills agenda with reference to problem-solving challenges and improving one's own learning and performance. It promotes the intrinsic value of enjoying and developing thinking, whilst learning examinable criteria and exploring ideas that may form the basis for GCSE learning and beyond.

All these developments need pupils to be aware of the 'thinking and learning' process they are going through. In this *New Key Geography Foundations* Teacher's Resource, 'thinking and learning' activities have been written to a teaching strategy that encourages pupil reflection on, and involvement in, their own learning process. Thus, 'thinking and learning' skills have been sensitively, deliberately and purposefully written into the material. Its approach is quite unlike other, traditional, worksheet-based resources and is innovative in its approach to encouraging independent learning. The 'thinking and learning' skills exercises:

◆ grow out of each unit in the *New Key Geography Foundations* pupil book double-page spreads
◆ introduce age-appropriate tasks and activities
◆ offer extension activities in addition to set tasks
◆ focus on the National Literacy Strategy's thrust to encourage literacy and learning across the curriculum
◆ use DARTs (Directed Activities Related to Texts) to their best advantage
◆ support extended writing through the use of writing frames and prompt sheets.

Literacy and learning

The KS3 National Strategy is the latest cross-curricular initiative to be introduced into schools in England. Its implementation ensures that geography teachers will be considering and planning how they will develop literacy objectives through their classroom. The *New Key Geography Foundations* Teacher's Resource supports this most recent trend in teaching geography and adds further value to the *New Key Geography* series. This focus will be timely. The National Literacy Strategy forms a teaching agenda rather than a set of assessment criteria and geography departments will have to consider this.

The search for a way to motivate pupils learning geography is one that has long engaged the skills, interest and imagination of teachers and educational writers. What is often overlooked is not so much *what* to teach but rather the principle of helping pupils *how* to learn. One concern was to present activity sheets that help to provide progression and reinforcement for a range of different abilities and individual teaching styles. Another factor was to recognise the difficulties faced by pupils, and to recognise the fact that they *can* succeed given the opportunity to do so. The principle of helping pupils *how* to learn is paramount, as is the development of encouraging strategies for *finding* information. There is the additional focus on presenting activities where the reader is engaged with material that focuses on the nature of the text itself and specifically on the promotion of 'reading for learning', with activities designed to direct active searching and critical reading. In today's curriculum there can be no place for activities that merely 'occupy' pupils and serve no real educational purpose.

Surely this must be the long-term objective of not only *teaching* geography, but also in helping pupils to *learn* geography, with an approach to using texts which focus on the nature of the text itself and which deliberately exploit the reader's capacity for processing and evaluating information.

Teaching, thinking and learning

One of the major problems facing today's geography teacher has been not only one of keeping abreast of the new ideas and approaches introduced through a developing National Curriculum, but also of introducing these new developments in the classroom. This emphasises the need for more work on teaching strategies and for resources at the right conceptual level. The traditional teaching approach of 'tell them (the pupils) what they're going to do, tell them to do it and then tell them what they've done' seems nowadays largely redundant. The *New Key Geography Foundations* Teacher's Resource promotes a four-phase generic framework to teaching and learning. The separate phases, although artificial, simply focus attention on aspects of the learning process that are present within any good lesson. In short, the structure provides both teaching clarity and impetus:

1 Setting the scene. Provide a general overview of the lesson and share learning objectives with the class.
2 New information. The teaching element of the lesson.
3 Processing. Where pupils learn to make sense of the information.
4 Review. An essential part of the experience. What has been learned? How has this been learned?

In essence this approach is not dramatically different to the didactic model; it merely serves to formalise what good teaching may already do but importantly it reflects the way in which the brain learns. There is the modelling provided by the teacher with guided activity for the learner followed with autonomous action by the learner:

◆ The brain is designed to cycle between receiving new information and making sense of it.
◆ Pupils find it easier to digest information and place it in context if they have been provided with the big picture prior to encountering detail.
◆ If pupils fail to review information, there is the inherent danger that significant amounts will be forgotten very quickly – around 40% within five minutes and 80% within 24 hours.
◆ If 15% of lesson time is devoted to thinking exercise, examination results improve.

This preferred structure is not designed to be restrictive nor prescriptive. It merely offers a flexible framework and not a rigid straight jacket. Teaching is very rarely precise and so interpretation will inevitably be very different in various situations. Even though the boundaries between these four phases will almost certainly be blurred, teachers will still be introducing new information and helping pupils understand it. Two aspects of the approach may be particularly appropriate:

1 An encouragement of what is being asked *of* the pupil, and awareness, *by* the pupil of the thinking processes and strategies adopted.
2 The importance placed on the fourth phase of any lesson – What has been learned? How this has been learned? – during which pupils can consider *what* they have achieved and *how* they went about it.

Enabling all pupils to benefit from the ordinary curriculum, and have access to it, will require considerable reflection on how traditional methods of teaching geography can be modified and approaches adapted.

The *New Key Geography Foundations* Teacher's Resource aims to offer some imaginative activities to teachers who are interested in promoting both active learning and critical thinking skills through *New Key Geography Foundations*. The activities are not simply aimed at pupils who excel at 'new' geography – a more intellectually rigorous subject than the more 'traditional' forms of geography. Rather, they introduce classroom-based resources that develop geographical skills and, in turn, allow access to an increasingly demanding curriculum. Recent research illustrates how most pupils perform better with 'teaching thinking' in their learning than they might have done without. It is not claimed that the activities in this resource cover all possible opportunities for encouraging pupils to *think* about thinking and learning *how* to learn. However, it does offer a number of teaching strategies that make learning more meaningful for pupils, improve understanding, help to reveal any pupil misconceptions, reduce anxiety and help teachers understand their subject matter.

Geography remains a challenging subject and an excellent vehicle for pupil-centred learning. However, there is a note of caution: the strategies presented in this file also include an element of risk. Teaching thinking does not encourage an 'anything goes' classroom climate but a level of debate and disagreement should be expected as pupils search for the best ideas and determine the outcome to probing activities. The activities are challenging, demand active participation, and offer variety, collaboration and hopefully real enjoyment. Activities address a developing National Curriculum and the range of preferred learning styles of pupils. They demand pupil involvement and collaboration making it more likely that geography teachers will be prepared to try out new ideas rather than retreat into the 'comfort zone' of traditional geography teaching. In time, they may go some way towards helping pupils become better thinkers and learners with geography lessons that remain vital and exciting.

In this new resource, 'directed-reading' activities and the *easier* 'thinking and learning' strategies have been sensitively, deliberately and purposefully written into the material. It is hoped that these resources will help to address the issue of not only providing accessible yet demanding classroom material, but of enhancing the role of reading in the secondary school geography curriculum.

In the long term, an increased awareness of thinking *for* learning should lead to improved performance, not just in geography, but through the pupils' whole experience both in and out of school.

It remains important that the wider educational debate about 'worthwhileness', 'relevance' and 'interest' are not ignored. If they are considered in the context of providing pupils with genuine opportunities for success, and in turn raising performance and standards of achievement, the rewards could be significant.

Assessment for Learning at Key Stage 3

Formative assessment or Assessment for Learning as it has become known has always been carried out by geography teachers. At times it has been undertaken by design, at other times automatically and instinctively. Today, it has developed a high profile owing to its introduction through the Foundation Subject strand of the National Strategy for Key Stage 3.

The National Strategy expects all schools to implement Assessment for Learning across the curriculum. For geographers, this highlights an opportunity to reassess current assessment practices and introduce new ones that build on existing structures. At its simplest, Assessment for Learning means that pupils are aware of what they can currently do and, crucially, discover what they need to know to improve.

According to Cowie and Bell (1999), 'Formative assessment is the process used by teachers and children to recognise and respond to pupil learning, in order to enhance that learning during the activity or task.' (Shirley Clarke (2005) *Formative Assessment in the Secondary Classroom*, Hodder Murray). During the 1990s, the government's focus was on summative assessment – measuring attainment or how well a pupil had done. The Assessment Reform Group, a group of assessment academics, decided to research whether this focus was correct. Paul Black and Dylan William, from King's College, University of London were commissioned to find out whether formative assessment could be shown to raise levels of attainment. They found that formative assessment strategies do indeed raise standards of attainment, with a greater effect for pupils of lower ability. At GCSE they were able to calculate an improvement of between one and two grades.

By introducing pupils to Assessment for Learning at Key Stage 3, teachers can train pupils to critically analyse the quality of their work and how it can be improved. Once embedded, these skills will help raise attainment throughout the key stage and onto GCSE.

Assessment for Learning with **NEW KEY GEOGRAPHY**

OFSTED published *Good Assessment in Secondary Schools* in 2003. A list of the areas of teaching and learning where formative assessment was deemed to be successful was provided. The list included:

◆ expected outcomes, discussed at the beginning of a topic or lesson

◆ a range of teaching methods that give pupils some responsibility for organising how they learn

◆ reflecting on the value of what has been achieved

◆ a collaborative approach to learning, with a strong emphasis on analysis and discussion

◆ an atmosphere that ensures pupils do not feel bad if they make a mistake.

By using the Assessment for Learning materials provided for *New Key Geography*, teachers will help to make the above a regular part of their classroom teaching.

The Assessment for Learning resources for *New Key Geography* have been designed with a number of principles in mind. These principles are derived from Black and William's research (Paul Black & Dylan William (1998) *Assessment and Classroom Learning* Assessment in Education: Principles, Policy & Practice Volume 5 Number 1 March, Carfax Publishing Limited: Oxfordshire, pp7–74):

◆ To provide effective feedback to pupils.

◆ To actively involve pupils in their own learning.

◆ To use assessment to motivate pupils to improve their learning.

◆ To empower pupils to be able to assess themselves and their peers.

◆ To enable pupils to recognise the next steps and how to take them.

Most of the suggested strategies involve pupils in assessment of their own work, in peer assessment, or in some form of discussion of their work either before, during or after it is attempted. All of these strategies are intended to increase pupils' awareness of what characterises good work, and how their own work can be developed and improved. The suggestions are not intended to be prescriptive. Rather, they provide teachers with opportunities that we consider fit the best practice of Assessment for Learning, and which target pupils' learning: an important area for focus in many OFSTED inspections.

One of the most important aspects of implementing Assessment for Learning is ensuring that pupils are given the necessary time to improve their work. This may be after drafting work or after work has been completed. Unless pupils can reflect on what they have achieved, and what they need to do to improve in future, the aims of Assessment for Learning will be lost.

Using the **NEW KEY GEOGRAPHY** Assessment for Learning resources

The assessment resources for *New Key Geography* have been designed to enable teachers to use them as flexibly as possible.

1   After pupils have been taught, activities from the pupil book undertaken and associated activity sheets from this resource completed, the **Assessment for Learning activities** can be used as a check on the learning and progress of the pupils. It is vitally important that pupils are clear what the next steps are in areas where they need to improve.

   Assessment for Learning activity sheets are provided for many, but not all, topics in the pupil book. These are to be found after the other activity sheets for each topic and are marked with an 'A' in the top right-hand corner of the sheet for easy recognition. While these activities have been developed specifically to be useful for assessment purposes, they can be used as equally valid activities alongside the other activity sheets.

   Suggestions are given for each unit on how to implement, differentiate and extend these Assessment for Learning activities, and how to get the most value from them.

   There are no activity sheets for Unit 1 What is geography? or Unit 7 Map skills. Instead, guidance is given to enhance particular activities in the pupil book or the activity sheets provided in this teacher resource.

2   The Assessment for Learning activities can be used at the end of a topic to check on the learning and progress of the pupils. This is not to suggest that they are a summative tool. The most important element of Assessment for Learning is acquiring the knowledge of how to improve in the future. This may be through reflecting on what constitutes a high-quality piece of work, so that these characteristics can be included when the next piece of work is attempted. Alternatively, it may be through looking at success criteria and ensuring that these criteria are met.

3   For each enquiry, at the end of each unit in the pupil book, pupils can be provided with the relevant **Checklist**. This will guide them in their work to ensure that they include all of the information required to complete the enquiry and present it in the correct manner to gain maximum marks.

4   After the unit enquiry has been completed, pupils can reflect on their progress using the **Think about your learning!** sheet. This gives them an opportunity to reflect on the skills they have developed, approaches which helped them succeed and barriers they encountered which stopped them from achieving their full potential. They are asked to think of targets to bear in mind for their next assessment, which will be added to by their teacher – collaboration in looking for ways to achieve success helps pupils feel more secure in looking to improve.

11

Assessment for Learning strategies

A number of strategies lend themselves particularly well to introducing Assessment for Learning in the classroom, many of which will be familiar already. With a little guidance, the power of these activities can be used to help pupils assess themselves or others formatively:

Self assessment

By asking pupils to critically evaluate their own work, they can see areas of success and those in need of development. Ensuring that the pupils can see the steps to improve areas of weakness is vital.

Peer assessment

A number of pupils are more likely to accept constructive criticism from their peers than they are from teachers! This method can take time to develop as there may be some initial discomfort from pupils about suggesting to their friends how they can improve. Given time and practice, peer assessment is a vital tool.

Success criteria

Giving pupils goalposts to aim at is clearly important. By giving them clear guidance, they are much more likely to achieve that success. In some cases the pupils themselves are asked to think of the success criteria either individually or as a group. This gives them greater ownership of the task and ensures they are all clear about what is expected of them if success is to be achieved.

Group discussions

By talking through ideas or answers, pupils clarify and check their own understanding. In this sense they are acting as checks and balances to each other. They are more likely to say what they really think in small groups rather than in front of the whole class and, therefore, their real ideas are processed and assessed.

Justifications

Explaining why pupils have decided upon a particular answer is a fundamental skill. Asking pupils to justify their answers to each other or to the whole class gives the teacher an opportunity to assess the quality of understanding as well as giving other pupils an opportunity to assess their own understanding against that of a peer.

Coaching

Pupils take on the role of teacher to teach small chunks of a topic to each other. By learning the material and then articulating it to others, the quality of understanding is deepened as well as being learned by others.

Assessment for Learning is about ensuring pupils know how to get from where they are to where they want to be. The Assessment for Learning materials in this *New Key Geography* Teacher's Resource will support them in making that progress.

Using attainment targets to produce assessments

Criteria in the level descriptors

The National Curriculum attainment target level descriptors for geography can be divided into three main criteria:

1 Place.
2 Environment.
3 Enquiry skills.

The place criterion can be further subdivided because, at Level 4 and beyond, an understanding of how geographical processes operate and how they affect places is part of the criterion. More details on the criteria are given in **Figures 1**, **2** and **3**.

Of course, assessing the level of any pupil involves finding a 'best fit' with the criteria as a whole. Pupils rarely perform in a uniform manner across all parts of all the criteria in a level. However, it is far more manageable and realistic to assess pupils under the different criteria before reaching a final judgement on their overall level of attainment.

FIGURE 1

Criteria 1a: **Recognising, describing and understanding places**

Level 1	They recognise and make observations about physical and human features of places.
Level 2	They describe physical and human features of places, recognising those features that give places their character. They show an awareness of places beyond their locality.
Level 3	They describe and make comparisons between the physical and human features of different localities. They offer explanations for the locations of some of those features. They show an awareness that different places may have both similar and different characteristics.
Level 4	They show their knowledge, understanding and skills in relation to studies of a range of places and themes at more than one scale.
	They begin to describe geographical patterns and to appreciate the importance of location in understanding places.
Level 5	They show their knowledge, understanding and skills in relation to studies of a range of places and themes at more than one scale.
Levels 6–8	They show their knowledge, understanding and skills in relation to a wide range of studies of places and themes, at various scales.

Criteria 1b: **Understanding geographical processes and how they affect places**

Levels 1–3	Not applicable to this criterion.
Level 4	They recognise and describe physical and human processes. They begin to show how these processes can change the features of places, and that these changes affect the lives and activities of people living there.
Level 5	They describe and begin to offer explanations for geographical patterns and for a range of physical and human processes. They describe how these processes can lead to similarities and differences between places. Pupils describe ways in which places are linked through movement of goods and people.
Level 6	They explain a range of physical and human processes. They describe ways in which the processes operating at different scales create geographical patterns and lead to changes in places.
Level 7	They describe the interactions within and between physical and human processes. They show how these interactions create geographical patterns and contribute to changes in places and patterns. They show understanding that many factors influence decisions made about places, and use this to explain how places change.
Level 8	They offer explanations for interactions within and between physical and human processes. They explain changes over time in the characteristics of places. They begin to account for disparities in development and show some understanding of the range and complexity of factors that contribute to the quality of life in different places.

Providing opportunities to meet the targets

It is unlikely that a single piece of work can allow pupils the opportunity to show their attainment in all the criteria at the same time. Levels of attainment can probably best be assessed using a variety of assessment methods. Sometimes traditional end-of-unit and end-of-term tests might be used to assess one or more of the criteria. Such tests can also fulfil many other functions, such as providing pupils with practice for the GCSE and other exams that they will meet later, and encouraging pupils to revise and consolidate work attempted earlier. They may also give pupils some satisfaction when they see the summative results of the work they have done in the preceding period.

However, other ways have to be found to assess pupils' levels of attainment. These can provide more and better opportunities to assess levels than traditional tests. In particular, they provide evidence for attainment in Criterion 3 – Enquiry skills.

In the edition of the *New Key Geography Foundations* pupil book, we have retained the enquiries at the end of each unit (except for Unit 1 What is geography? and Unit 7 Map skills). Teachers might choose to use these as class exercises and provide guidance on how the enquiry should work. On other occasions, pupils will be asked to work as independently as possible.

When a great deal of teacher guidance is given, the enquiry may still allow pupils to show attainment of the enquiry criterion at some of the lower levels. However, they will only be able to attain the higher levels when they are allowed to work on their own and to develop their own routes to enquiry. In fact, as it is assumed that *New Key Geography Foundations* will be used by pupils at the start of Key Stage 3, the book provides carefully structured guidance on how to carry out the enquiries. As the book and the series progresses, the level of guidance is reduced and pupils are encouraged to plan their own enquiries. This allows them the opportunity to move gradually on towards the higher levels of attainment.

FIGURE 2

Criteria 2	**Appreciating the environment and understanding its management**
Level 1	They express their views on features of the environment in a locality that they find attractive or unattractive.
Level 2	They express views on attractive and unattractive features of the environment of a locality.
Level 3	They offer reasons for some of their observations and judgements about places.
Level 4	They describe how people can both improve and damage the environment.
Level 5	They offer explanations for ways in which human activities affect the environment and recognise that people attempt to manage and improve environments.
Level 6	They describe and offer explanations for different approaches to managing environments and appreciate that different approaches have different effects on people and places.
Level 7	They appreciate that people's lives and environment in one place are affected by actions and events in other places. They recognise that human actions may have unintended environmental consequences and that change sometimes leads to conflict.
Level 8	They recognise the causes and consequences of environmental issues and show understanding of different approaches in tackling them. They understand and apply the concept of sustainable development.

Figure 3

Criteria 3	**Carrying out geographical enquiries**
Level 1	They use resources provided, and their own observations, to respond to questions about places.
Level 2	They select information from resources provided. They use this information and their own observations to respond to questions about places. They begin to use appropriate vocabulary.
Level 3	They use skills and sources of evidence to respond to a range of geographical questions.
Level 4	They draw on their knowledge and understanding to suggest suitable geographical questions for study. They use a range of geographical skills drawn from the Key Stage 3 Programme of Study, and evidence to investigate places and themes. They communicate their findings using appropriate vocabulary.
Level 5	They identify relevant geographical questions. Drawing on their knowledge and understanding they select and use appropriate skills, from the Key Stage 3 Programme of Study, and evidence to help them investigate places and themes. They reach plausible conclusions and present their findings both graphically and in writing.
Level 6	Drawing on their knowledge and understanding, pupils identify relevant geographical questions and suggest appropriate sequences of investigation. They select and make use of a wide range of skills, from the Key Stage 3 Programme of Study, and evidence in carrying out investigations. They present conclusions that are consistent with the evidence.
Level 7	With growing independence, pupils draw on their knowledge and understanding to identify geographical questions, establish a sequence of investigation, and select and use accurately a wide range of skills, from the Key Stage 3 Programme of Study, and evidence. They are beginning to reach substantiated conclusions.
Level 8	Drawing on their knowledge and understanding, pupils show independence in identifying appropriate geographical questions and implementing an effective sequence of investigation. They select and use effectively and accurately a wide range of skills, from the Key Stage 3 Programme of Study, and evidence to reach substantiated conclusions.

Assessing levels of attainment using *New Key Geography* enquiries

When enquiries have been completed, teachers must assess them against relevant criteria from the level descriptors. They cannot be used for assessing the complete level of attainment. Therefore, teachers need to make templates, selecting from the criteria provided in the National Curriculum order. An example of a detailed template has been provided here. This can be used for assessing attainment in the United Kingdom enquiry on pages 122–123 in the pupil book.

Levels of attainment mark scheme for the UK enquiry

The enquiry, as described in the pupil book, can allow pupils to exhibit *some* of the characteristics of the levels of attainment from Level 2 to Level 5. These characteristics are described below, using phrases taken from the geography level descriptions. If the instructions to pupils are developed and extended, it should be possible for them to show some of the characteristics of higher levels of attainment. With some added support, the less able should be able to show some characteristics of Level 1.

When assessing the completed work, and the process that led to that work being completed, teachers should assess which of the descriptions below best fits the work that is being assessed.

Level 1   Pupils make observations about the features of places.
They use resources provided and their own observations to respond to questions about places.

Level 2   Pupils describe features of places, recognising those features that give places their character.
Pupils select information from resources provided.
They ask and respond to questions about places.
They begin to use appropriate vocabulary.

Level 3   Pupils describe and make comparisons between features of different localities.
They offer reasons for some of their observations and judgements about places.
They use skills and sources of evidence to respond to geographical questions.

Level 4   Pupils show their knowledge, understanding and skills in relation to studies of a range of places.
They use a range of geographical skills and evidence to investigate places.
Pupils draw on their knowledge and understanding to suggest suitable geographical questions for study.
They communicate their findings using appropriate vocabulary.

Level 5   Pupils show their knowledge, understanding and skills in relation to studies of a range of places.
Pupils describe ways in which places are linked through the movement of people.
Pupils identify relevant geographical questions.
Drawing on their knowledge and understanding, they select and use appropriate skills to help them investigate places.
They reach plausible conclusions and present their findings both graphically and in writing.

Level 6   Pupils show their knowledge, understanding and skills in relation to studies of a wide range of places.
Drawing on their knowledge and understanding, pupils identify relevant geographical questions and suggest appropriate sequences of investigation.
They select and make effective use of a wide range of skills and evidence in carrying out investigations.
They present conclusions that are consistent with the evidence.

Level 7   Pupils show their knowledge, understanding and skills in relation to studies of a wide range of places.
They show understanding that many factors influence decisions made about places.
With growing independence, pupils draw on their knowledge and understanding to identify geographical questions, establish a sequence of investigation, and select and use accurately a wide range of skills and evidence.
They are beginning to reach substantiated conclusions.

Level 8   Pupils show their knowledge, understanding and skills in relation to studies of a wide range of places.
Drawing on their knowledge and understanding, pupils show independence in identifying appropriate geographical questions and implementing an effective sequence of investigation.
They select and use accurately a wide range of skills and evidence to reach substantiated conclusions.

Assessment with the NEW KEY GEOGRAPHY enquiries

For each enquiry there is a **Checklist**. These are designed to provide pupils with success criteria so that they have a clear idea of what is expected if they are to produce high-quality answers and improve future performance. The Checklists can be used in two ways:

1   They can be used by pupils to check whether or not they have met the success criteria for the enquiry. As they complete each task they can tick off the parts they have completed. If there are any parts not ticked off, pupils can be sure of what they need to include to complete the enquiry satisfactorily.

2   The Checklist can also be used by an assessor (either a teacher or another pupil if an element of peer marking is to be introduced) to mark pupils' work. Once again, the boxes that remain empty will diagnose where the pupil has failed to meet the criteria. The work could be returned to the pupil once an assessor has looked at the work so that any omissions can be corrected by the pupil. This process of drafting and improving work is an important skill for geographers and will breed good habits for future years.

The **Think about your learning!** assessment sheet, provided for each unit, gives an opportunity for pupils to reflect on the work they have undertaken during the enquiry. By considering how they approached a task, pupils can compile a list of their own success criteria and analyse barriers to their learning. This information will leave them better prepared to approach the enquiry in the following unit.

Assessment for Learning in NEW KEY GEOGRAPHY Foundations

Assessment for Learning activities and support, in the form of teacher's notes are provided for every unit in the pupil book. These activities are in the form of photocopiable sheets, and are integrated with the other activity sheets for each spread in the pupil book.

The assessment activity sheets are marked with an 'A' in the top right-hand corner for easy recognition. While these activities have been developed specifically to be useful for assessment purposes, they can also be used as equally valid activities alongside the others.

Pupil book page	Topic	Assessment activity provided	Teacher's Resource page
1 What is geography?			
No assessment activity sheets are provided for this introductory unit. Suggestions are given for how Assessment for Learning can be implemented in this topic using activities in the pupil book.			
4–5	What is geography? Your passport to the world		
6–7	What is physical geography?		
8–9	What is human geography?		
10–11	What is environmental geography?		
12–13	How do we study geography?		
14–15	How can we find out where places are?		
16–17	How can we use graphs in geography?		
18–19	How can we use computers in geography?		
20–21	What is the value and use of geography?		
2 Weather and climate			
22–23	Weather and climate – How can the weather affect us?		
24–25	How might you observe and record the weather?	✓	45
26–27	How can local features affect temperature and wind?	✓	48
28–29	What is Britain's weather?	✓	50
30–31	How does it rain?	✓	54–56
32–33	Forecasting the weather – anticyclones	✓	58
34–35	Forecasting the weather – depressions	✓	60
36–39	The weather enquiry	✓	63
3 River flooding			
40–41	River flooding – Why is flooding a problem?		
42–43	How does the water cycle work?	✓	72
44–45	What is a river basin? Where are the world's most important rivers?	✓	74
46–47	What causes a river to flood?	✓	76
48–49	Floods in the UK, 2000	✓	79–80
50–51	How does the UK cope with floods?	✓	85
52–53	Floods in Bangladesh, 2004		
54–55	How does Bangladesh cope with floods?	✓	90
56–57	How can the risk of flooding be reduced?	✓	93
58-59	The river flooding enquiry	✓	96

1 What is geography?

KEY IDEAS:

◆ differences between physical, human and environmental geography
◆ finding places on a map

◆ using maps and photos to describe places
◆ how to understand and appreciate geography
◆ the value and use of geography.

PoS	Key questions	Pupil book	Suggested activities/methods
1	What is geography?	4, 5	Discuss with pupils their prior learning of geography from their previous school/phase of education.
1	What is physical geography? What is human geography? What is environmental geography?	6, 7 8, 9 10, 11	Discussion with pupils to find out their ideas as to 'what is geography'? Use model landscapes to identify and define natural and human environments. Consolidation by games.
2d	How can places be recognised and described using oblique aerial photos?	12	What is the meaning of 'place'? Use of key words, photos and fieldsketches to describe 'places'.
2b, 2c, 2e	How can places be described on a labelled fieldsketch?	13	Compare an urban and rural landscape. Label fieldsketches.
2c	What are the main lines of latitude and longitude?	14, 15	Use of a globe and an atlas.
2c	How can the globe be shown as a flat surface?	14	Try to lay the peel of an orange flat onto a sheet of paper.
2c	How can latitude and longitude be used to find places in an atlas?	15	Using the index of an atlas and locating countries on a world map.
2e	How can information be shown on different graphs and how are these graphs interpreted?	16, 17	Recognition of bar graphs, line graphs, pie graphs and scatter graphs. Interpretation and use of these graphs.
1f, 2e, 2f, 2g	How can we use computers in geography?	18, 19	Visit the *Key Geography* website. In the section on Key Stage 3 links, go to the 'ICT Activities'. Try, for example, an internet-based 'places quiz', at http://www.triv.net/qmenu.htm
1	What is the value and use of geography?	20, 21	Taking each theme (environmental geography, etc.), ask pupils to suggest at least one way in which geography is of use to people.

PoS	Skills	Vocabulary and technical terms			
2c	Atlas index/contents	*(see Glossary in pupil book)*			
2c	Latitude and longitude	Atmosphere	Hazard	Physical geography	Settlement
2d	Oblique aerial photos	Climate Communications	Landforms Landscape	Pollution Population	Resources River basin
2d	Annotated fieldsketch	Drought	Latitude	Primary activities	Tertiary activities
1f, 2e, 2f, 2g	ICT, use of website	Ecosystem Environment	Longitude Migration	Quality of life Secondary activities	Urban Weather
		Fieldsketch	Place	Service activities	

Assessment for Learning

No activity sheets have been provided for Unit 1 as it is an introductory unit. Instead, guidance is given below to enhance particular activities in the pupil book.

There are a number of opportunities to implement Assessment for Learning strategies within this unit.

Pages 6–7: Activities 1 and 2

These activities provide an opportunity for pupils to work in pairs. If they are asked to discuss and agree which statement is the odd one out, it is likely that the understanding of the pupils will deepen as a result of the discussion. If they disagree, the discussion undertaken to come to an agreement is an excellent way for pupils to articulate their thoughts, reassess their ideas and formulate new opinions. If a whole class discussion takes place about some of the sets of words, then the process is repeated.

Pages 12–13: Activity 5

This activity provides an opportunity for peer assessment and drafting of work. Once the pupils have written their description and drawn their map, another pupil can mark their work with constructive criticism. This will provide both pupils with new ideas by reading other pupils' work, give them an idea of the standard of other pupils' work in the class and provide them with ways to improve. Once they have had time to improve their own work, the overall standard will have risen.

Geography – your passport to the world

You can't ignore geography – it's all around you! Without geography you're
nowhere! People go places with geography! Wherever you live in the world,
you are also a global citizen. You are one of over six billion people who live
on planet earth – and the number is growing. You are connected to people
and places all over the world in a variety of ways.

 Design a geography slogan for the blank T-shirt below.

 List 10 ways in which you can learn about other places.
Here are two to get you started:

  ◆ a pen-pal in another country   ◆ a story in a newspaper.

 Make a list of places you have visited in the UK and abroad.
The visit must have been for longer than a day.

Your passport to the world

Geography is about people and places. It helps us to understand our world and makes it a more interesting place in which to live. You are connected to people and places all over the world in a variety of ways – even through the clothes you wear. It's time to investigate your wardrobe!

1   Add your favourite clothes to the sketch below. You can include shoes, sportswear and even your school uniform!

2   Find the clothing labels, usually stitched into a seam, and discover where in the world your clothes were made.

3   Label the outline sketch to show how the clothes you wear connect you to people and places all over the world. Write the names of the items in boxes, together with the names of the countries where they were made.

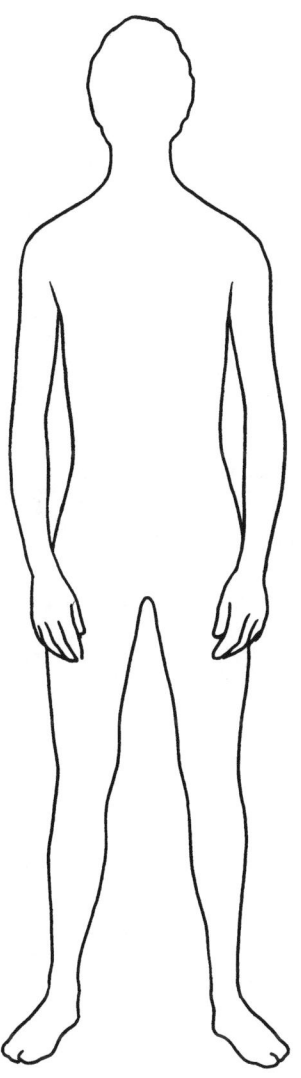

4   Find out how many of your clothes are made in LEDCs. Locate these countries on an outline map of the world and label the map to show how your wardrobe connects you to people and places all over the world.

How can we find out where places are?

Every day we are influenced by the world around us. Places we hear about, food we eat, people we meet and the clothes we wear. You are connected to people and places all over the world in a variety of ways.

 On a copy of the map below, show how you are connected to different places around the world. Think about:

- your friends
- things you buy
- music you listen to
- sports
- relatives

- pen-pals
- TV programmes you watch
- newspapers/magazines you read
- learning a foreign language
- clothes

- holidays
- books you read
- the internet
- cars
- food

 Write the names or labels in boxes around the map.

 Draw an arrow from each box to its country.

 How many places have you actually visited? How many of your connections are through people, rather than through possessions?

What is physical geography?

Physical geography is the study of the earth's natural features. It is about the land, the sea and the atmosphere around us.

 Label as many physical features as possible in the sketch below. It has been started for you. You may wish to check your answers by looking at pages 6 and 7 in the pupil book.

Snow covered mountain.

 Think about your journey to school in the morning. Name **five** physical features that you pass.

◆ _____

◆ _____

◆ _____

◆ _____

◆ _____

What is physical geography?: Odd one out

Physical geography is the study of the earth's natural features. It is about the land, the sea and the atmosphere around us.

Below is a list of words to do with physical geography.

1	Storms.	**11**	Mountain.	**21**	Volcano.
2	Thunderstorm.	**12**	Earthquake.	**22**	Clouds.
3	Hurricane.	**13**	Flood.	**23**	Ice.
4	Rock.	**14**	**Landforms**.	**24**	Sea.
5	Volcanic eruption.	**15**	**Climate**.	**25**	Cliff.
6	Rainfall.	**16**	Plants.	**26**	Soil.
7	**Weather**.	**17**	**Natural hazards**.	**27**	Vegetation.
8	Snow.	**18**	Drought.	**28**	Waterfall.
9	Rivers.	**19**	Air.	**29**	Beach.
10	Temperature.	**20**	**Earth's surface**.	**30**	Marsh.

a Working with a partner, study the sets of numbers below, which match to words in the list above.

b Cross out the 'odd one out' in each set.

c Add a fourth number to match the other two.

d Explain what links the three 'in' numbers.

Set A	4	27	26	
What's the link?				
Set B	9	13	5	
What's the link?				
Set C	27	12	26	
What's the link?				
Set D	21	28	25	
What's the link?				
Set E	1	8	14	
What's the link?				
Set F	7	15	4	
What's the link?				
Set G	22	18	8	
What's the link?				

 Sort all the words from the list above into groups, using the words in **bold** as headings.

What is human geography?

Human geography is the study of where and how people live. It is also about people and places and how they affect each other. Geography can help us to understand our world and, hopefully, make it a better place in which to live.

 Label as many human features as possible in the sketch below. It has been started for you. You may wish to check your answers by looking at pages 8 and 9 in the pupil book.

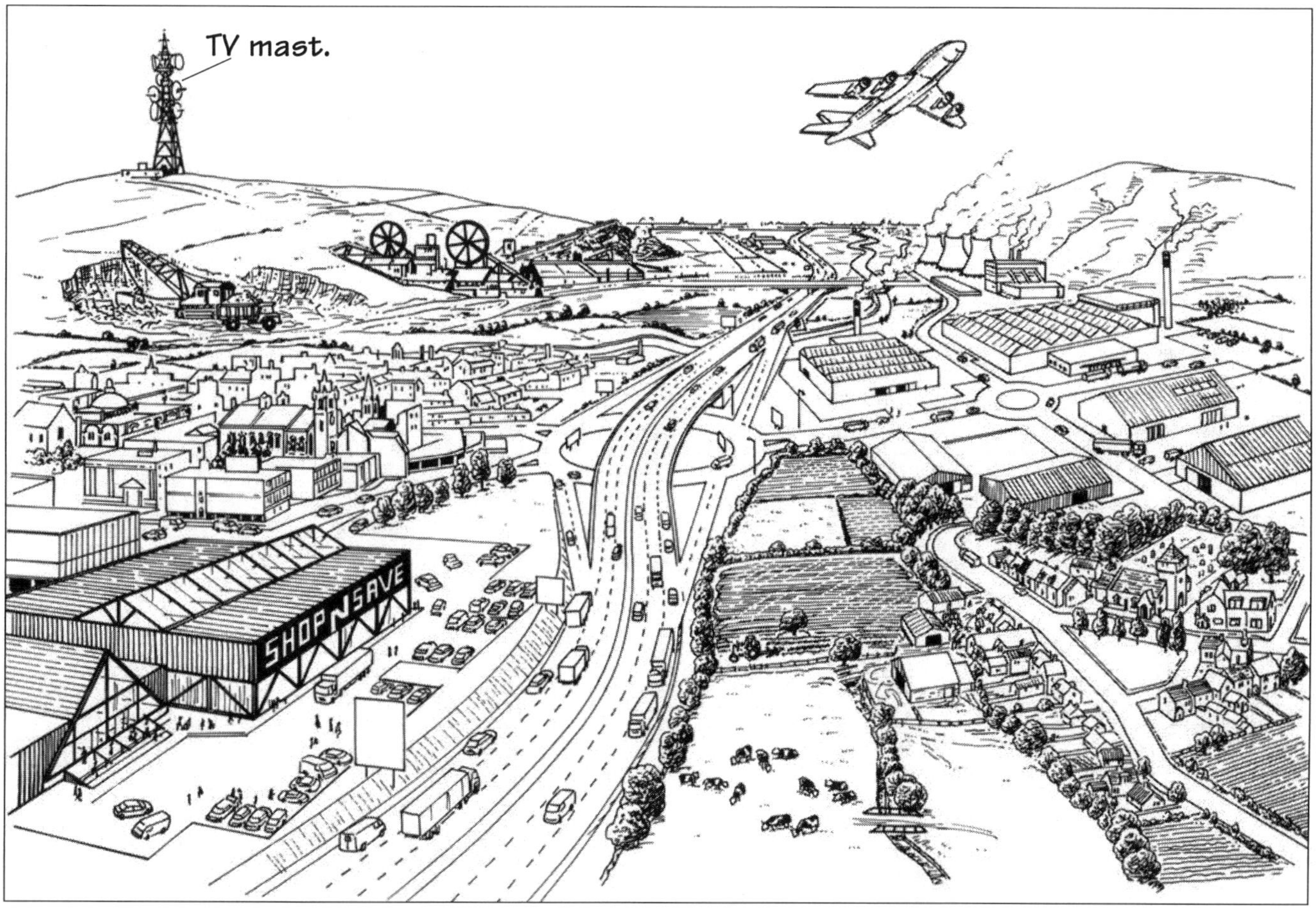

TV mast.

SHOP N SAVE

2 Think about your journey to school in the morning.
Name **five** human features that you pass.

◆ _____

◆ _____

◆ _____

◆ _____

◆ _____

What is human geography? Odd one out

Human geography is the study of where and how people live. It is also about people and places and how they affect each other. Geography can help us to understand our world and, hopefully, make it a better place in which to live.

Below is a list of words to do with human geography.

1	TV mast.	12	Motorway.	23	Farming.
2	Large city.	13	Town.	24	Education.
3	Industry.	14	Imports.	25	Vehicles moving people and goods.
4	Trade.	15	**Quality of life**.		
5	Mining and quarrying.	16	Distribution.	26	Jobs.
6	Migration.	17	**Communications**.	27	Transport.
7	**Settlement**.	18	Small village.	28	Rural.
8	Trade.	19	Exports.	29	Aeroplane.
9	Urban.	20	**Economic activity**.	30	Factory.
10	Money.	21	Health.	31	**Population**.
11	Shopping.	22	Life expectancy.		

 a Working with a partner, study the sets of numbers below, which match to words in the list above.

b Cross out the 'odd one out' in each set.

c Add a fourth number to match the other two.

d Explain what links the three 'in' numbers.

Set A	1	29	18	
What's the link?				
Set B	22	9	2	
What's the link?				
Set C	12	23	5	
What's the link?				
Set D	14	13	25	
What's the link?				
Set E	8	16	6	
What's the link?				
Set F	24	21	29	
What's the link?				
Set G	22	18	8	
What's the link?				

 Sort all the words from the list above into groups, using the words in **bold** as headings.

What is environmental geography?

Environmental geography is the combination of the physical environment of climate, landforms, soils and vegetation, and the human environment which includes settlements and economic activities. It is the study of the surroundings in which people, plants and animals live.

 1   Label as many environmental features as possible in the sketch below. It has been started for you. You may wish to check your answers by looking at page 10 in the pupil book.

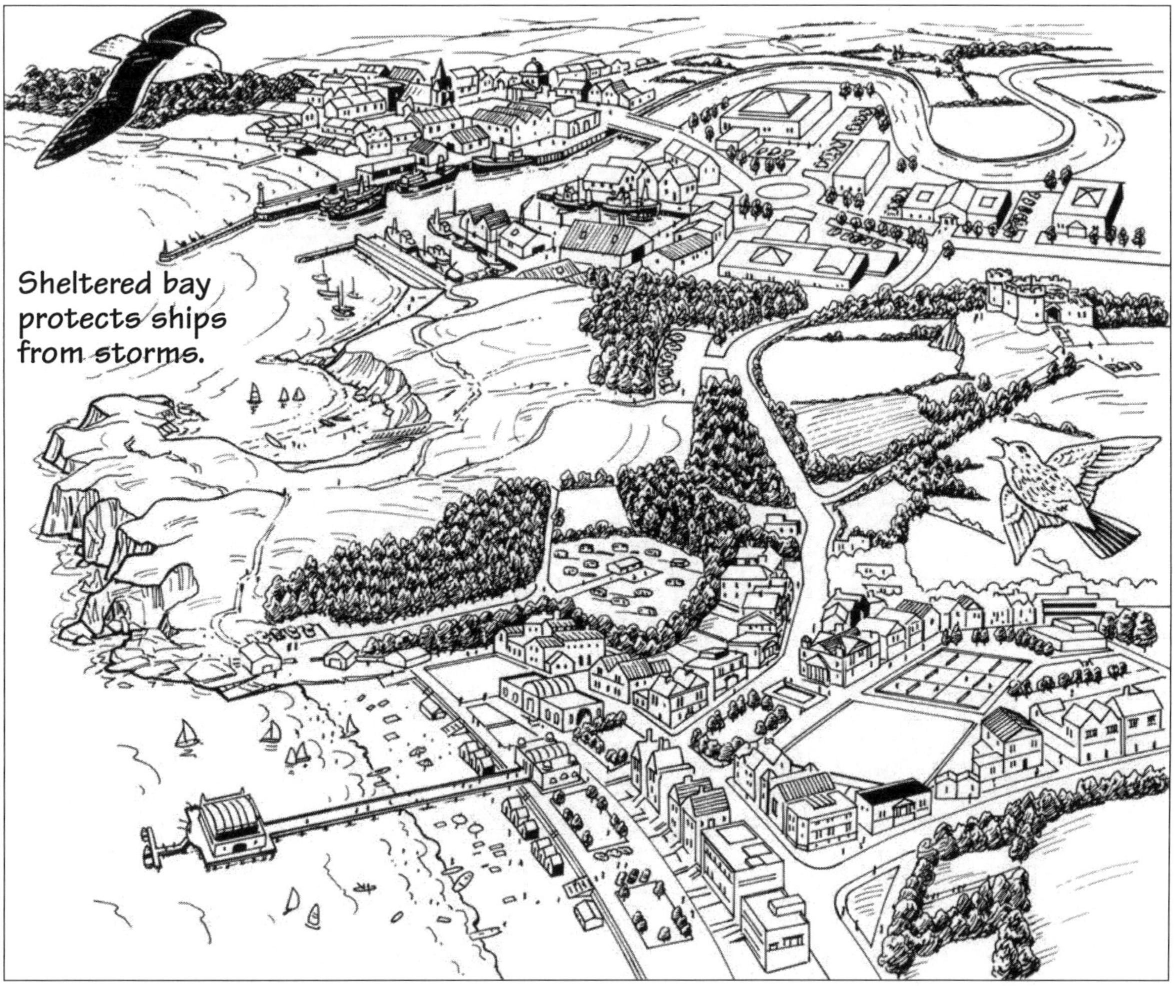

Sheltered bay protects ships from storms.

2   Think about your journey to school in the morning. Name **five** environmental features that you pass.

◆ _____

◆ _____

◆ _____

◆ _____

◆ _____

What is environmental geography?

Environmental geography is the combination of the physical environment of climate, landforms, soils and vegetation, and the human environment which includes settlements and economic activities. It is the study of the surroundings in which people, plants and animals live.

 Label as many environmental features as possible in the sketch below. It has been started for you. You may wish to check your answers by looking at page 11 in the pupil book.

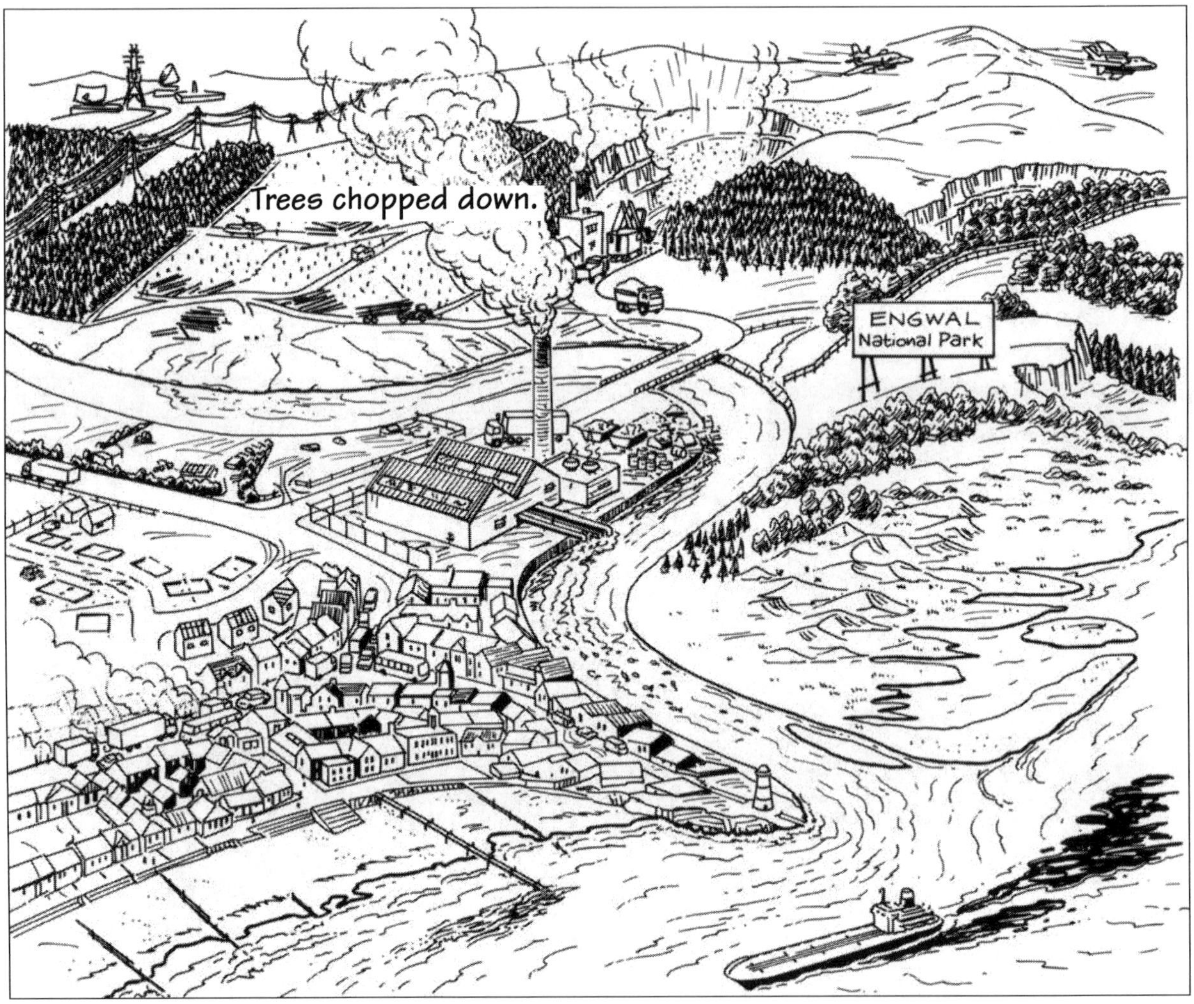

Trees chopped down.

ENGWAL National Park

2 Think about your journey to school in the morning. Name **five** environmental features that you pass.

◆ _____

◆ _____

◆ _____

◆ _____

_____

How the environment is improved, destroyed and spoiled

Environmental geography is the combination of the physical environment of climate, landforms, soils and vegetation, and the human environment which includes settlements and economic activities. It is the study of the surroundings in which we live.

 Read what geographers say about the environment below.

Nature reserves are homes for animals.

Recycle garden and household waste.

New roads and houses are built which destroy farmland.

Cutting down the rainforests allows the rain to wash away the soil.

Litter is dropped on streets.

Traffic noise spoils the peace and quiet.

Use lead-free petrol.

Dirty rivers can kill fish.

Smoke from factories pollutes the atmosphere.

Laws stop factories making pollution.

Oil in the sea and litter spoils beaches.

Planting trees improves the view.

Cleaning up rivers helps fish.

Car and lorry fumes pollute the air.

The ozone layer is being destroyed.

Untreated waste from factories kills fish.

Saving energy stops oil being used up.

 Colour each statement as follows:

◆ Use **green** if the statement describes how the environment is **improved**.

◆ Use **red** if the statement describes how the environment is **destroyed**.

◆ Use **blue** if the statement describes how the environment is **spoiled**.

How do we study geography?

 Study the pictures below and the photos on the front cover of your text book.

What time of day is this?

Why is it like this?

What is the purpose of this development?

Who drew this picture and why?

How is it changing?

Does this picture tell the whole story about this place?

Who is affected by the changes?

What is going on in this picture?

What might happen in the future?

How did this place get to be like this?

How do people feel about it?

Where is this place?

Why is this happening?

How do I feel about it?

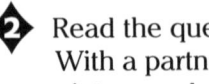 Read the questions asked about the pictures. With a partner, discuss what you see in each picture and answer the questions in **bold**.

 Share your ideas with your partner. Is it possible to interpret the same picture in different ways?

 Ask your partner at least two more questions about what you see in each picture.

How do we study geography? Asking questions

1 Study the photo below, which has been taken from the front cover of the pupil book.

What time of day is this?

Why is it like this?

What is the purpose of this development?

Who took this photo and why?

How is it changing?

Does this photo tell the whole story about this place?

Who is affected by the changes?

What is going on in this photo?

What might happen in the future?

How did this place get to be like this?

How do people feel about it?

Why is this happening?

How do I feel about this place?

Where is this place?

What is it like?

2 With a partner, read the questions asked about the photo. Discuss what you see in the photo and answer the key questions in **bold**.

3 On a large copy of the table below, name the physical, human and environmental features in the photo.

Physical features	Human features	Environmental features

4 Photos do not tell the whole picture about a place. What features cannot be read from a photo?

How can we find out where places are?

Maps are useful to people. They help us to find out where places are and what they are like. An atlas shows many places around the world. These places may be easily found using latitude and longitude.

Imagine you have won a holiday leaving London and flying to five cities across the world. However, you have not been told where you are going. Instead, the travel company has sent you a text message that uses latitude and longitude coordinates and you have to find out for yourself!

Congratulations! You've won a holiday visiting five cities.

Leave London on Saturday	Fly to 40°N	4°W (city A)
Leave city A on Sunday	Fly to 30°N	31°E (city B)
Leave city B on Tuesday	Fly to 41°N	12°E (city C)
Leave city C on Thursday	Fly to 6°N	3°E (city D)
Leave city D on Friday	Fly to 36°S	57°W (city E)
Leave city E on Saturday	Fly back to London	

 1

  a Find out which cities you will be visiting by using the latitude and longitude coordinates.

  b Using a coloured pencil, plot the flights on to the world map below.

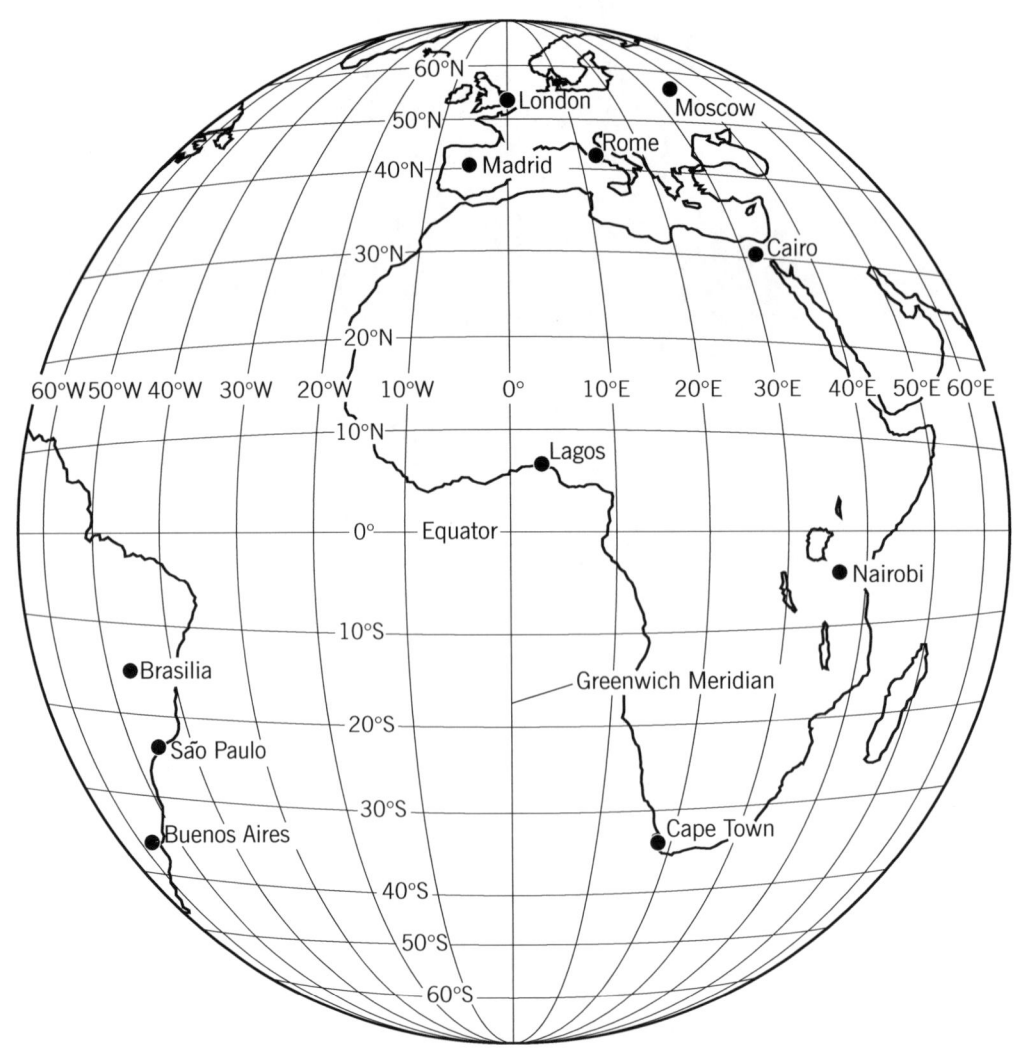

How can we find out where places are?

Maps are useful to people. They help us to find out where places are and what they are like. An atlas shows many places around the world. These places may be easily found using **latitude** and **longitude**.

 Write a sentence below about each of the cities you will visit saying what country and continent each is in.

◆ _____

_____

◆ _____

_____

◆ _____

_____

◆ _____

_____

◆ _____

_____

 A friend of yours has won a similar holiday! This trip must visit five different cities to your holiday.

a Using a different coloured pencil, plot the trip on the world map by starting and finishing in London.

b Write a text message, similar to the one on Activity Sheet 1.13a using latitude and longitude coordinates.

3 In your book or file, write a sentence about each of the cities your friend will visit saying what country and continent each is in.

4 If you could visit any city in any country on any continent, where would you go? Explain your choice.

What is the value and use of geography?

The knowledge and skills that you learn in geography can help you to understand our world and can be of help to you in future years.

 Read what pupils say about geography and colour questions about:

◆ physical geography in **blue**

◆ human geography in **red**

◆ environmental geography in **green**

◆ skills in geography in **yellow**.

Why must we learn to live in a sustainable way?

How can maps and photos help me to find out what places are like?

How can I get to know the world through fieldwork?

Why are countries at different stages of development?

What are some of the problems facing our world and how might we solve them?

Will I use computers and other technology to find things out and present information?

How can we prepare for and cope with natural hazards?

How can I learn to understand other cultures?

How can the world be made a better place for everyone?

What are the important questions, issues and problems we are facing?

Why are there different living standards around the world?

What are the different environments like and where are they found?

Why do different people have different views about how to use the environment?

Why must we recycle waste materials and reduce energy consumption?

Will the skills I learn in geography help me in a job?

 Think about what you have already learned about geography.
Copy out any **four** questions above and write an answer for each one.

2 Weather and climate

Unit Overview

Approximate teaching time, 12 hours

KEY IDEAS:

- observing and recording the weather
- how local features affect temperature and wind
- what causes rain

- how weather and climate vary across Britain
- anticyclones and depressions
- forecasting the weather.

PoS	Key questions	Pupil book	Suggested activities/methods
6d	How can the weather affect us?	22, 23	Discuss with pupils how the weather has affected them over a certain period of time, for example a week.
6d	What simple methods can be used to observe and record the weather?	24, 25	Brainstorm weather definition. Describe how weather can be measured. Work in pairs on observing and recording. Homework – keep a weather diary for five days.
6d iii	How can temperature and wind be affected by local conditions?	26, 27	Describe climate differences in a small area. Explain the causes of these differences. Group work – school microclimate enquiry. Homework – home microclimate enquiry.
6d i	What are the meanings of the terms weather and climate?	28	Define terms, emphasise difference and support with examples.
6d iii	How and why does temperature and rainfall in the British Isles vary from place to place and season to season?	28, 29	Map interpretation to show spatial and seasonal differences. Simple explanation of differences using five main reasons. Construction of map to show four main climate areas of Britain.
6d iii	How can rising air cause rainfall and how do relief, convection and fronts each produce rain in this way?	30, 31	Simple diagram to show how it rains. Define precipitation and condensation. Simple diagrams and explanations to show the main rainfall types. Compare data showing Britain's rainfall and high ground to confirm the link.
6d iii	How is the weather of the British Isles affected by anticyclones and depressions?	32–35	Brainstorm the value of weather forecasts. Use photos to show how satellite images can help weather forecasters.
1	How can the enquiry process be used to identify differences in weather and climate across Britain?	36–39	Pupils undertake a geographical enquiry to desribe and explain geographical variations in Britain's weather and climate.

PoS	Skills
1	Undertaking a geographical enquiry
2	Classify information
2	Describe a distribution pattern
2	Present and interpret data
2b	Measure and record weather
2b	Collect data from outside the classroom
2c	Points of the compass
2c	Observe and record
2d	Relate satellite images to weather maps
2d	Interpret satellite images

Vocabulary and technical terms

(see Glossary in pupil book)

Anticyclone	Depression	Precipitation
Aspect	Frontal rain	Pressure
Beaufort scale	Isobar	Relief rain
Climate	Meteorology	Temperature
Condensation	Microclimate	Visibility
Convectional rain	North Atlantic Drift	Weather

Assessment for Learning

Pages 24–25: Activity Sheet 2.7

Encourage pupils to think in pairs about what a successful weather report would include. The success criteria for this answer would include commenting on temperature, precipitation, wind speed, wind direction, cloud cover and the use of appropriate geographical terminology. Ensure enough time is allocated for pupils to reflect on the success criteria.

Follow this up by asking pupils to peer assess each other's work using the success criteria as a guide to marking. Allocate more time to allow pupils to edit their answers in the light of the peer assessment.

Differentiation
Differentiate the activity by allowing/not allowing pupils access to the pupil book.

Extension
Extend pupils' answers by asking them to reflect on places that may exhibit this particular kind of weather.

Pages 26–27: Activity Sheet 2.10

Encourage pupils to think individually about what a successful answer would include. The success criteria for this answer would include commenting on surface, shelter, aspect, buildings and the use of appropriate geographical terminology. Ensure enough time is allocated for pupils to reflect on the success criteria before they begin writing their answers.

Differentiation
Differentiate the activity by giving pupils a number of sites to choose from around the school.

Extension
Ask pupils to justify why they would not choose another site around their school. If appropriate, pupils should refer to physical features in their school locality.

Pages 28–29: Activity Sheet 2.12

Model a perfect answer to question 1 at the front of the class. Pupils can use this as a framework for completing answers to questions 2 and 3.

Differentiation
Remove some of the data from the table and ask pupils to predict what the missing data is likely to be.

Extension
Pupils should choose the region in which they live and explain why their region receives the type of climate shown in the table.

Pages 30–31: Activity Sheets 2.16a–c

Ask pupils to self or peer assess their work by researching any corrections using pages 30–31 in the pupil book.

Differentiation
Give pupils a word box containing all of the missing labels for Activity Sheets 2.16a and b. The labels are: Warm moist air; Warm air rises; Condensation occurs and clouds form; Air descends; Rain stops; Ground is warmed by the sun; Air cools; Precipitation occurs. Some labels can be used in more than one answer.

Extension
Ask pupils why Fort William receives 2,000 mm of rainfall per year but London only receives 610 mm. Award credit for accurately labelled diagrams as part of the answer.

Pages 32–33: Activity Sheet 2.18

Choose a pupil to justify the location of one of the statements. Write their answer on the board. Ask other pupils to improve the answer by adding/removing words. Alternatively, ask other pupils to counter argue the first pupil's answer.

Differentiation
Reduce the activity to just characteristics of either a summer or winter anticyclone.

Extension
Give pupils extra statements to add to their diagrams such as: Sun high in the sky; River levels fall; Hosepipe bans likely; Extra coastguards are employed; Sun low in the sky; There are more likely to be road traffic accidents; Water pipes may burst; and Football matches are cancelled.

Pages 34–35: Activity Sheet 2.20

Ask pupils to work in pairs and to justify their choice of answer in turn. Once the pupils have completed the activity sheet, use traffic lights to survey the class. Group together pupils who are green to coach those who are red or amber.

Differentiation
Remove one of the incorrect labels from each box.

Extension
Remove all of the labels from the table.

Pages 36–39: The weather enquiry

The weather enquiry Checklist (page 63) can be used in two ways.

1 It can be used by pupils to check whether or not they have met the success criteria for the enquiry. As they complete each task, pupils can tick the parts they have completed. If there are any parts not ticked, pupils can be sure of what they need to include to complete the enquiry.

2 The Checklist can also be used by an assessor (either a teacher or another pupil if an element of peer marking is to be introduced) to mark pupils' work. Once again, the boxes that remain empty will diagnose where the pupil has failed to meet the criteria. The work could be returned to the pupil once an assessor has looked at the work so that any omissions can be corrected by the pupil. This process of drafting work is an important skill for geographers and will breed good habits for future years.

The Think about your learning! assessment sheet (page 64) provides an opportunity for pupils to reflect on the work they have undertaken during the enquiry. By considering how they approached a task, pupils can compile a list of their own success criteria and analyse barriers to their learning. This information will leave them better prepared to approach the enquiry in the following unit.

How does weather affect us?

Weather affects our lives in many ways. It can affect the sort of activities we do, the type of clothes we wear, what we plan to do at the weekend and where and when we go on holiday.

State how each of the following people is likely to be affected by the weather and climate in the UK.

The owner of an ice-cream parlour in Blackpool.

_____

_____

_____

A farmer in East Anglia.

_____

_____

A lifeguard on a beach in Devon.

_____

_____

The owner of a ski resort in Scotland.

_____

_____

A Park Ranger in the Lake District National Park.

_____

_____

_____

A fisherman on a trawler in the North Sea.

_____

_____

_____

A teenager on a day trip to a theme park.

_____

_____

_____

How can the weather affect us?

Weather affects our lives in many ways. It can affect the sort of activities we do, the type of clothes we wear, what we plan to do at the weekend and where and when we go on holiday.

Below are two weather maps for one day in August.

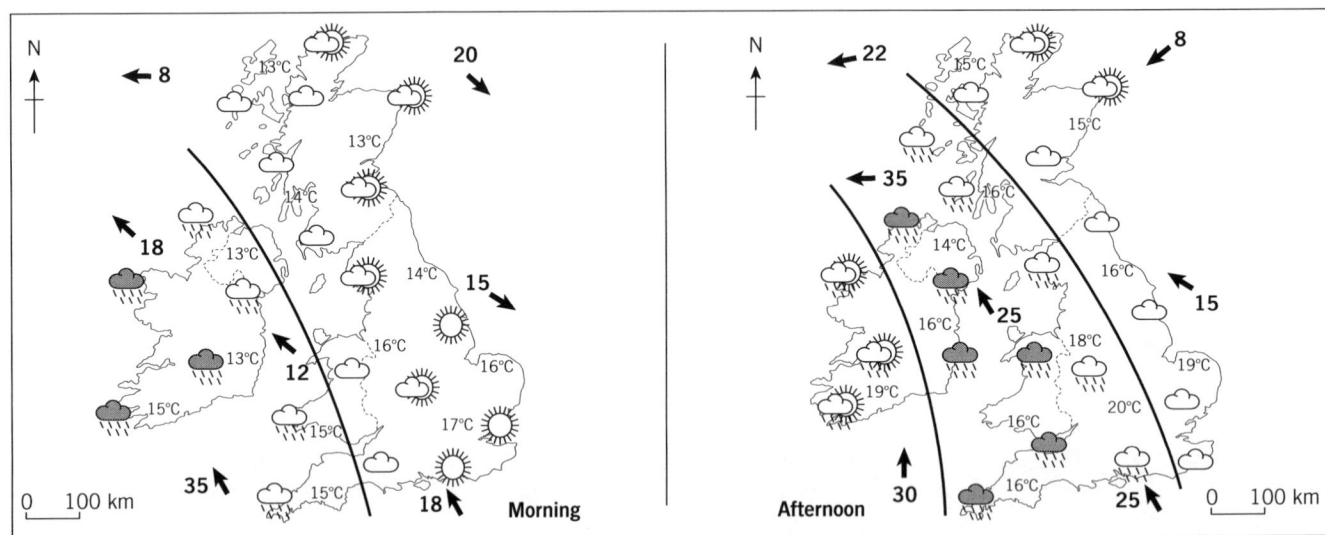

1 With reference to the maps above, answer the following questions. Give reasons for your answers. You may need to use an atlas.

Q Is a full day's play at the Oval cricket ground in London likely today?

A _____

Q Will wet weather or slick tyres be needed for Formula 1 motor racing at Silverstone today?

A _____

Q Will lifeguards allow body-boarders in the water in Newquay today?

A _____

Q Will a farmer in Suffolk cut the grass for silage today, or should he wait until tomorrow?

A _____

Q Will an ice-cream seller be busy in Great Yarmouth today?

A _____

Q If you lived in Birmingham and fancied a day out today, which National Park would you go to, Snowdonia or the Lake District?

A _____

Q Would you take the ferry from Dover for a day-trip to France today?

A _____

 Think of three more questions and try them out on a partner.

How can the weather affect you?

Weather affects our lives in many ways. It can affect the sort of activities we do, the type of clothes we wear, what we plan to do at the weekend and where and when we go on holiday.

Look at the pictures below. In your book or file, write how each type of weather might affect you.

The weather – good or bad news?

Weather affects our lives in many ways. It can affect the sort of activities we do, the type of clothes we wear, what we plan to do at the weekend and where and when we go on holiday.

 Read the newspaper headlines below. With a partner, decide whether each headline gives good or bad news.

 Colour what you would consider to be the good news in green and the bad news in red. Be careful, this is not as easy as it may first appear!

Fog closes airport

'Monsoon' storm floods city

Blizzards hit Scotland

Hottest summer on record

Phew, what a scorcher!

English resorts hotter than Spain

Church struck by lightning

The big freeze goes on...

1000s die in flash floods

Sunbathers risk skin cancer in summer sun

Rain stops play

Heavy rain brings record sales of umbrellas

Ferry crossings cancelled by storm

Fog causes motorway madness

Harvesting hampered by waterlogged fields

Forest fires spread across the USA

Trains stopped in their tracks by leaves on railroad

Sunstroke victims in casualty

Worst storms on record

Floods cause devastation

Mudslides destroy village

Worst storms for 100 years

Summer hosepipe ban

Britain colder than Siberia

Investigate the weather further by collecting articles about it from newspapers and the internet. Why did the weather make the news in each article you collected?

Hurricane hits UK

Gales batter east coast

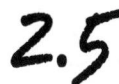
How might you observe and record the weather?

The weather maps shown on TV are based on thousands of weather
observations made around the world. Weather forecasting is very
scientific. It uses satellites, weather balloons, ships, aircraft, radar
and some of the most powerful computers in the world.

 Colour the matching heads and tails below.

Heads   **Tails**

| Civil and military aircraft | and sea measure wind, rainfall, temperature and more. |

| Weather stations on land | report as they travel the world. |

| Satellites | measure winds, temperature and humidity in the sky. |

| Weather balloons | show where it is raining. |

| Weather radars | in space send back pictures of clouds. |

 A weather scientist (or meteorologist) needs the following
measurements in order to describe the weather.
Colour the matching pairs below.

How hot or cold it is.	Visibility.
The weight of air pressing in on us.	Hours of sunshine.
Rain, snow, hail or sleet.	Wind direction.
How 'wet' the air is.	Cloud cover.
Measured in kilometres per hour.	Rainfall.
Where the wind blows from.	Wind speed.
Measured in eighths.	Relative humidity.
Measured by a sunshine recorder.	Pressure.
How far we can see.	Temperature.

 Watch the weather forecast on TV or on the
Met Office website (www.met-office.gov.uk).
In your book or file, write a paragraph to
describe tomorrow's weather. Use the title:
'Here is the weather forecast...'

Observing and recording the weather

Weather is the day-to-day condition of the atmosphere. A simple record of the weather may be made by careful study of what is going on around us.

 1 The box below contains a list of words to do with watching and recording the weather. Working with a partner, write each word only once around the words in **bold** on the right. It has been started for you. Cross each word off as you go.

Foggy	*Rain*
~~Rain~~	
Clear sky	**Precipitation**
Very cold	
Stratus	
Thermometer	
Fresh gale	
Thunder	**Cloud type**
Wind vane	
Snow	
Showers	
Hail	
Cloudy	**Cloud cover**
Warm	
Fog	
Cumulus	
Calm	**Wind speed**
Sunny	
Mild	
East	
Strong breeze	
Mist	**Wind direction**
Poor	
North	
Hot	
Sleet	
Cirrus	**Temperature**
Total cloud cover	
Cumulonimbus	
Fair	
Eighths	**General weather**
Beaufort scale	
Good	
Bright	

 2 What is the weather like today? Look at the words on your diagram. Underline the words that describe today's weather.

 3 Compare your description with other pupils' in your class. You could read them out to one another. Are they similar or different?

And today's weather is...

    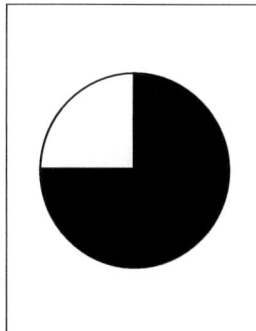

The *Middleton Gazette* is looking for a new reporter to write a daily weather report. You have decided to apply for the job.

As part of your application you have been asked to write a detailed description of the weather using the cartoons above.

_____

_____

_____

_____

_____

_____

_____

_____

_____

_____

_____

_____

_____

_____

_____

_____

_____

_____

_____

_____

_____

_____

How can local features affect temperature and wind?

Site conditions such as aspect, shelter, physical features and other factors can influence temperature, local wind speed and direction.

When the climate in a small area is different to the general surroundings, it is called a **microclimate**. Below is a list of words to do with microclimates.

1	South facing.	**13**	Hills.	**25**	Hill tops.
2	Physical features.	**14**	Seas.	**26**	Cool.
3	Light surface.	**15**	Wind speed.	**27**	Stored heat.
4	Buildings.	**16**	Shelter.	**28**	Surface.
5	Facing the sun.	**17**	Walls.	**29**	Warmer.
6	Aspect.	**18**	Lakes.	**30**	North facing.
7	Office block.	**19**	Trees.	**31**	Thermometer.
8	Tarmac.	**20**	Shade.	**32**	Wind strength.
9	Schools.	**21**	Facing the wind.	**33**	Eighths.
10	Hedges.	**22**	Dark surface.	**34**	Light.
11	Shelter from wind.	**23**	Grass.	**35**	Heavy.
12	Soil.	**24**	Light winds.	**36**	Metres.

 a Working with a partner, study the sets of numbers below, which match to words in the list above.

     b Cross out the 'odd one out' in each set.

     c Add a fourth number to match the other two.

     d Explain what links the three 'in' numbers.

Set A	19	18	8	
What's the link?				
Set B	25	7	4	
What's the link?				
Set C	11	12	17	
What's the link?				
Set D	12	8	27	
What's the link?				
Set E	1	5	21	
What's the link?				

 Sort all the words from the list above into groups, using the following headings:
Physical features, **Buildings**, **Shelter**, **Surface**, and **Aspect**.

Investigating the weather around your school

Site conditions such as aspect, shelter, physical features and other factors can influence temperature, local wind speed and direction. When the climate in a small area is different to the general surroundings, it is called a microclimate.

Carry out a survey of the weather (or microclimate) around your school.

Below are the steps you should follow in carrying out your survey.

Step 1
Questions to ask
Suggest some ideas and questions that could be used to help investigate the weather around your school, e.g:
- Where are the warmest places?
- Where are the windiest places?
- Where are the coldest places?

Step 2
Guesswork
What predictions can you make about the answers to your questions before you even start?

Step 3
Data collection
- What data and information will you need to collect?
- How will you collect it?
- What equipment will you need?
- Where will you collect your data?

Step 4
Observation
- Take measurements at your selected sites.
- Check your observations by repeating them.

Step 5
Results
- Use a variety of methods to show your results.
- Include a plan of your school.
- Use tables, charts and graphs.
- Show differences between selected sites.
- Use ICT – word process your work. Use a database or spreadsheet. A PowerPoint presentation would be really impressive!

Step 6
Conclusions
- What have you found out?
- Use your results to draw conclusions.
- State whether your results prove/disprove your predictions.
- Explain your findings by using your new knowledge and understanding of the microclimate around your school.

Where would you build an outdoor social area in your school?

The head teacher of your school has given you a sum of money to build an outdoor social area.
Describe where you would build the social area and explain why you have chosen this site.

What is Britain's weather?

Britain may be a small area of land but the climate varies from place to place and from season to season.

 Study the events listed below. They all took place in a town called Lowestoft in Suffolk. Each event is linked to the climate recorded on the graph.

A Lesley has to scratch the ice off her windscreen before she leaves for work.

B Lucy can't go out on her bike, as it's just too dark and wet after school.

C Taylor decides to go to the beach for a swim and play Frisbee.

D Phew! It's so hot that Paige decides to sunbathe using a factor 25 sun cream.

E Janet decides to take her jacket out with her just in case it rains.

F Callum has to play hockey on the Astroturf, not on the school playing field.

G Michael wants to go and fly his new kite.

H Susan hangs her washing out to dry on the washing line, as it's a warm day.

I Craig decides to wear his waterproof boots on the geography field trip.

J Jim arrives late for work, the flood water led to long road diversions.

K Steve's old car won't start first thing in the morning.

L Beth isn't going to school today because it's closed due to heavy snowfall.

 Using the climate graph, match each event in the list above to one of the months below.

January =	May =	September =
February =	June =	**October** =
March =	**July** =	November =
April =	August =	December =

 Think of four sentences to describe each of the months shown in **bold** above.

The weather across the UK

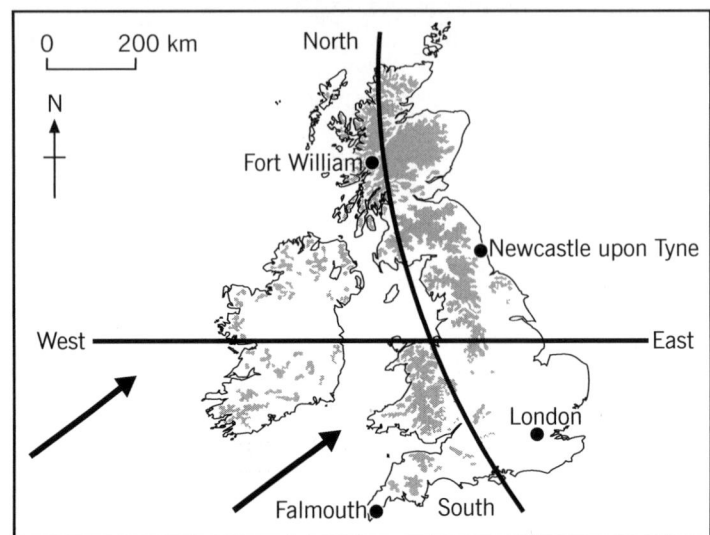

Location	Average summer temperature	Average winter temperature	Altitude (metres above sea level)
Fort William	13	5	10
Newcastle upon Tyne	14	4	45
London	16	5	20
Falmouth	16	7	10

1 Explain why Falmouth is the warmest location in winter.

_____

_____

_____

2 Explain why Fort William is the coolest location in summer.

_____

_____

_____

3 Explain why Newcastle is the coolest location in winter.

_____

_____

_____

Relief rainfall

Rain is caused by moist air rising and cooling. The three types of rainfall produced in this way are relief, convectional and frontal.

Relief rainfall is quite common in Britain especially in the west where most of the high land is located.

The statements below describe what happens when we get relief rainfall. Number the statements in the correct order. It has been started for you. Add your numbers to the correct places on the sketch below.

Order	
	The other side of the high land (the leeward side) stays dry and sheltered.
1	Warm, moist air is blown in from the sea.
	When this moist air reaches high land, it can do only one thing: it has to go up.
	As the air rises, it cools.
	Droplets in the cloud join together to form larger droplets, which fall as rain.
	The rain falls on the high land (the windward side) facing into the wind.
	As it cools down, the water vapour in it condenses to form tiny water droplets.
	The wind meets a line of high hills or mountains.
	The tiny droplets of water form clouds.

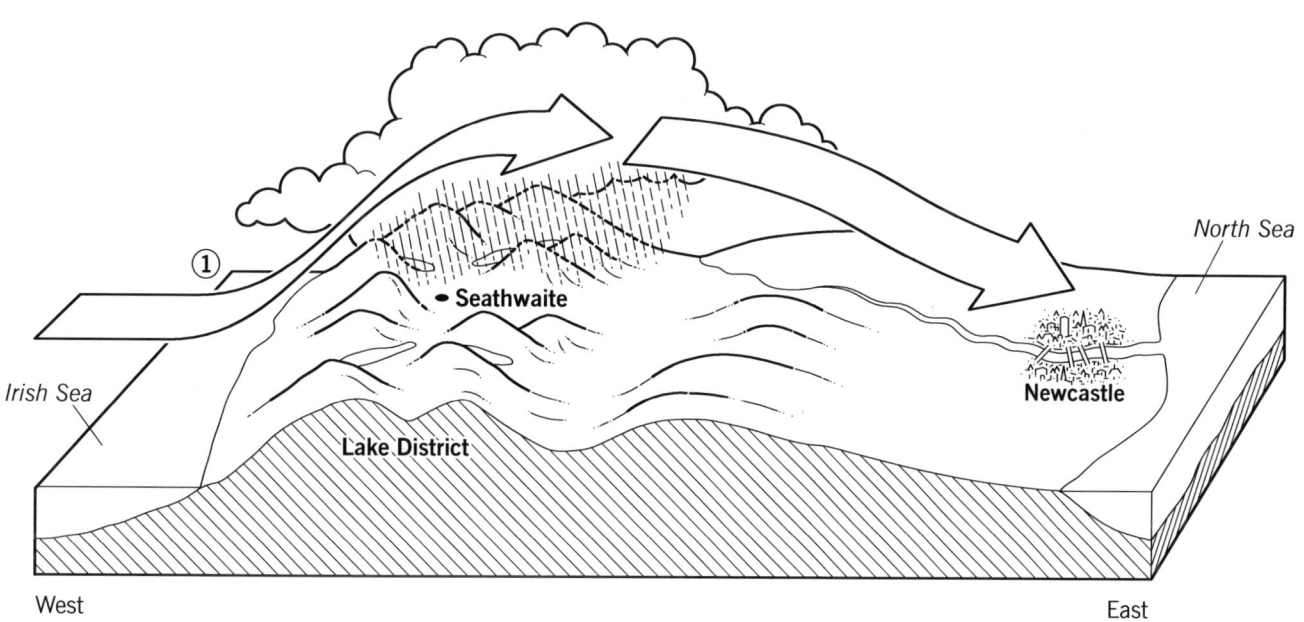

Convectional rainfall

Rain is caused by moist air rising and cooling. The three types of rainfall produced in this way are relief, convectional and frontal.

Convectional rainfall is more likely to form in the summer than in the winter and is more likely to fall inland than on the coast.

The statements below describe what happens when we get convectional rainfall. Number the statements in the correct order. It has been started for you. Add your numbers to the correct places on the sketch below.

Order	
	As it cools down, the water vapour in it condenses to form tiny water droplets.
	This warm air rises as a convection current.
1	On very warm days the sun's heat warms the ground.
	As the air rises, it cools.
	The tiny droplets of water form clouds.
	The air above the ground is warmed.
	Sometimes the convection currents are very strong and produce very tall clouds and heavy rainfall with thunder and lightning.
	Droplets in the cloud join together to form larger droplets, which fall as rain.

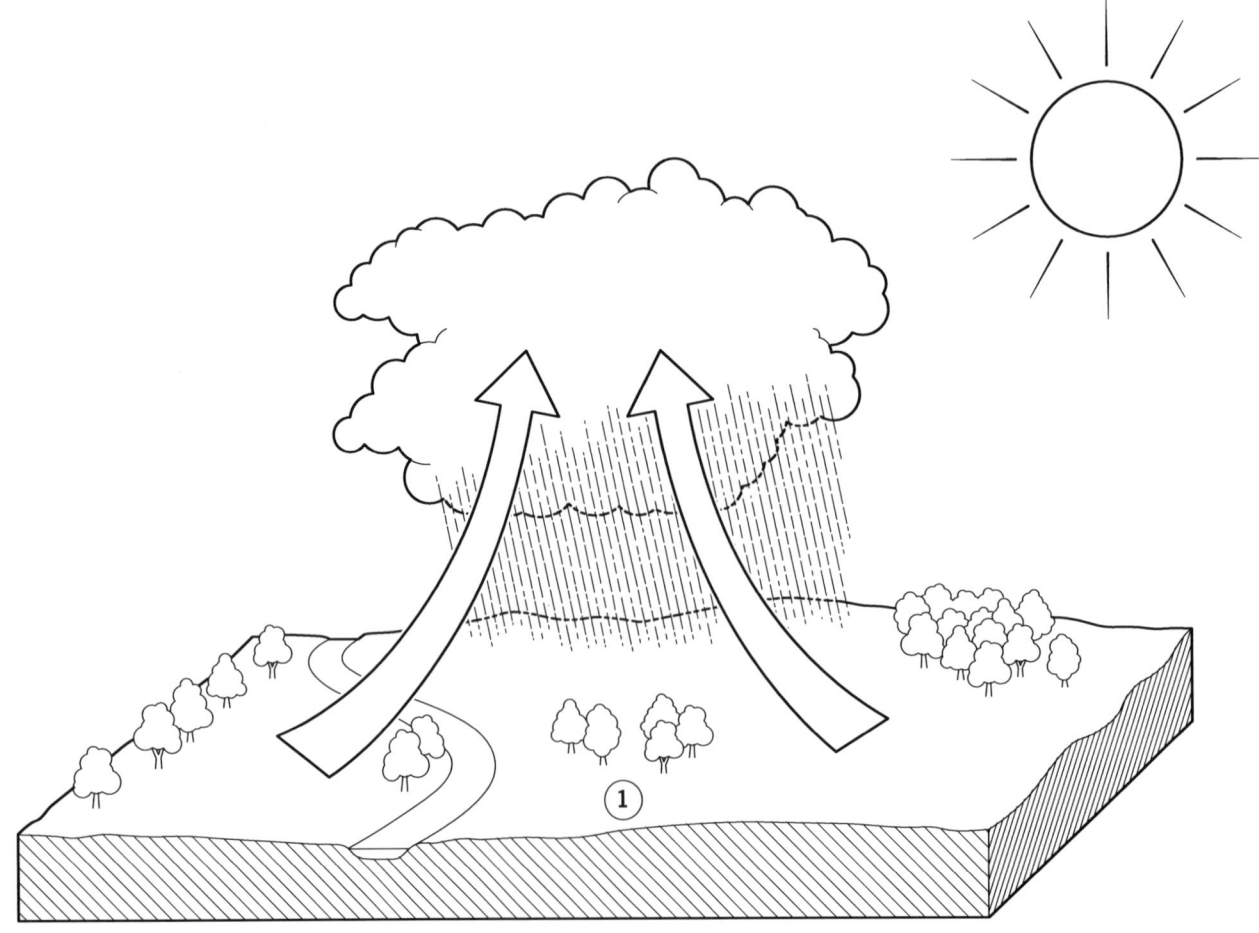

Frontal rainfall

Rain is caused by moist air rising and cooling. The three types of rainfall produced in this way are relief, convectional and frontal.

Huge blocks of air at different temperatures move around the earth over sea and land. The place where warm air and cold air meet is called a front. Frontal rainfall is very common in Britain throughout the year and especially in winter.

The statements below describe what happens when we get frontal rainfall. Arrange the statements into the correct order and label the sketch.

Order	
	As it cools down, water vapour in it condenses to make tiny water droplets.
	Droplets in the cloud join together to form larger droplets, which fall as rain.
	At the front, the lighter warm air rises up and over the colder, heavier air.
	As the warm air rises, it cools down.
	The zone where they meet is called a front.
1	Sometimes a mass of warm air meets a cold one.
	The tiny droplets of water form a gently sloping bank of clouds.
	When warm air and cold air meet, they do not mix.

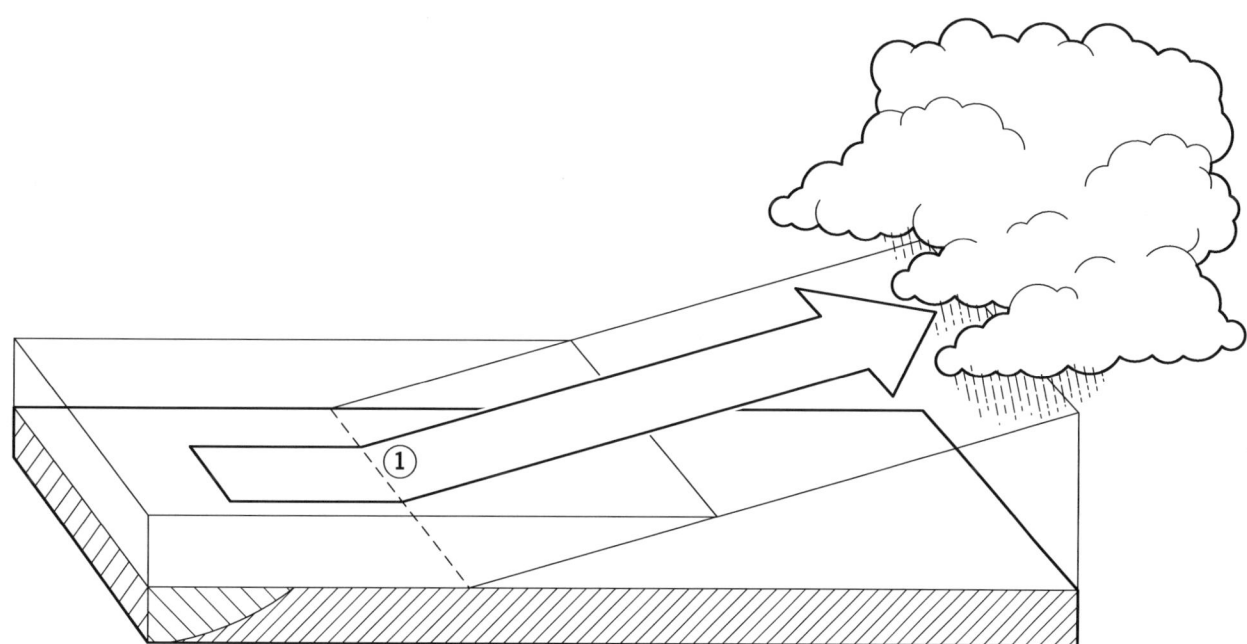

What type of rainfall?

Complete the diagram below by writing labels in
each of the five boxes. Also complete the title.

Title _____

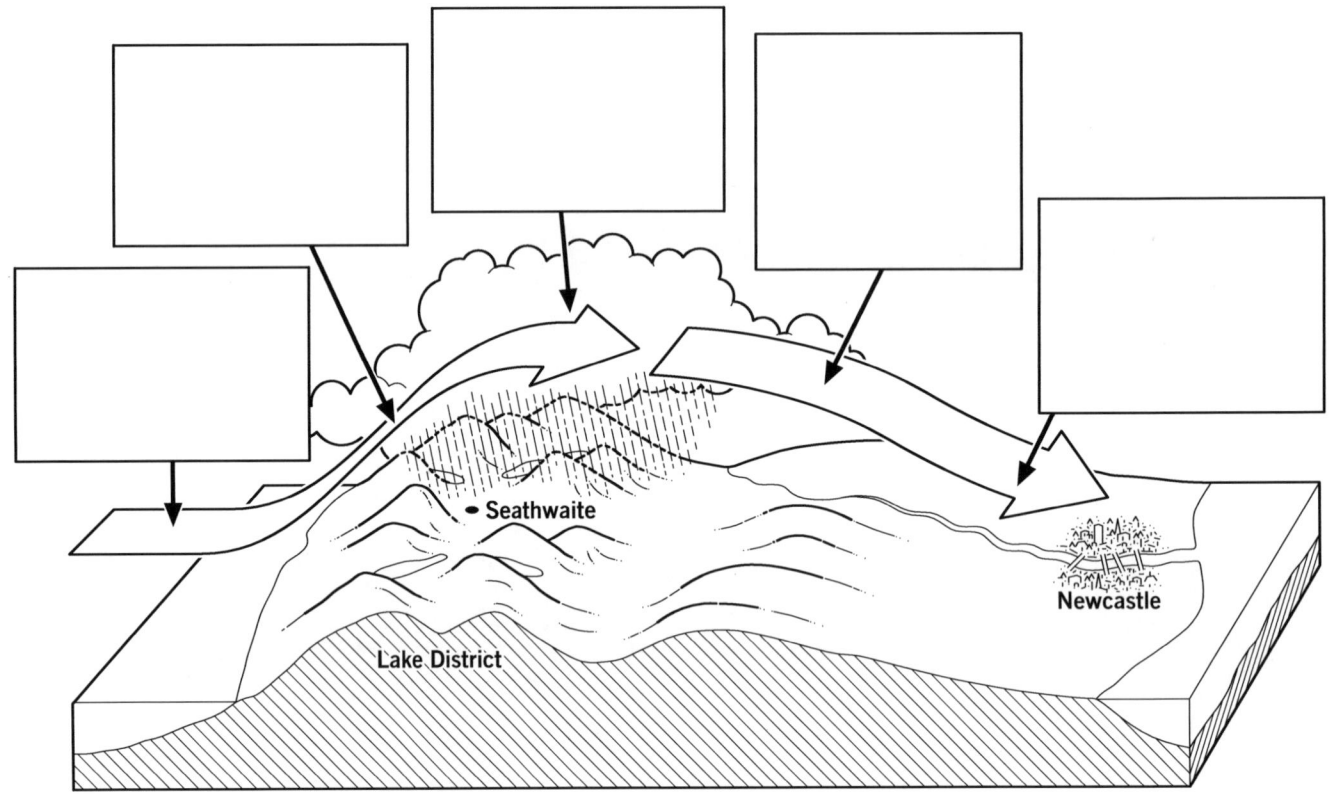

What type of rainfall?

1 Look at the image. Name the type
of rainfall that would occur in a
place like this:

_____

2 Complete the flow chart below to show how this type of rainfall occurs.

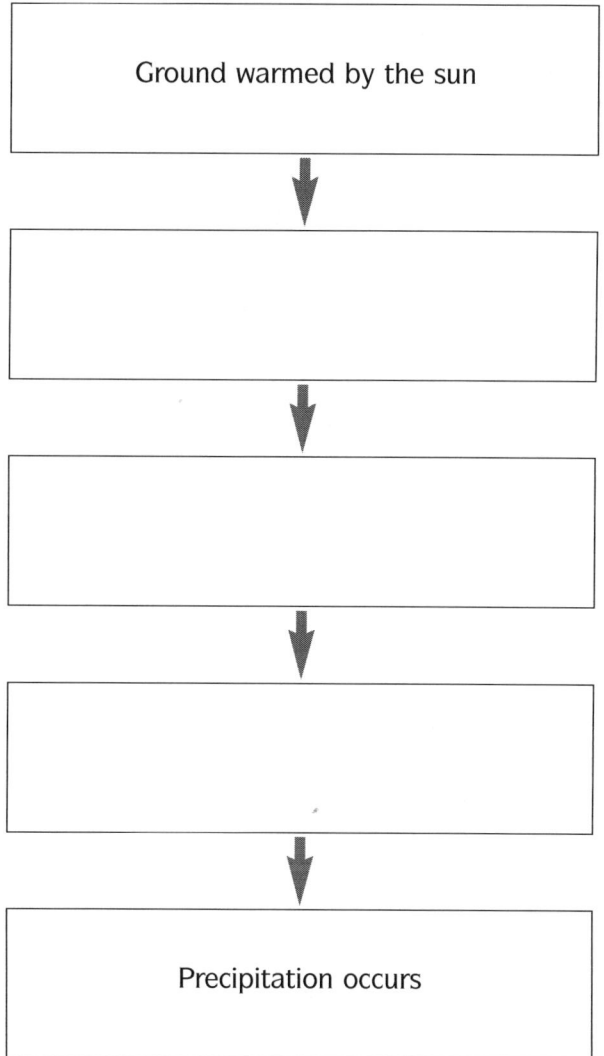

Ground warmed by the sun

Precipitation occurs

What type of rainfall?

 Look at the diagram below. Name this type of rainfall: _____

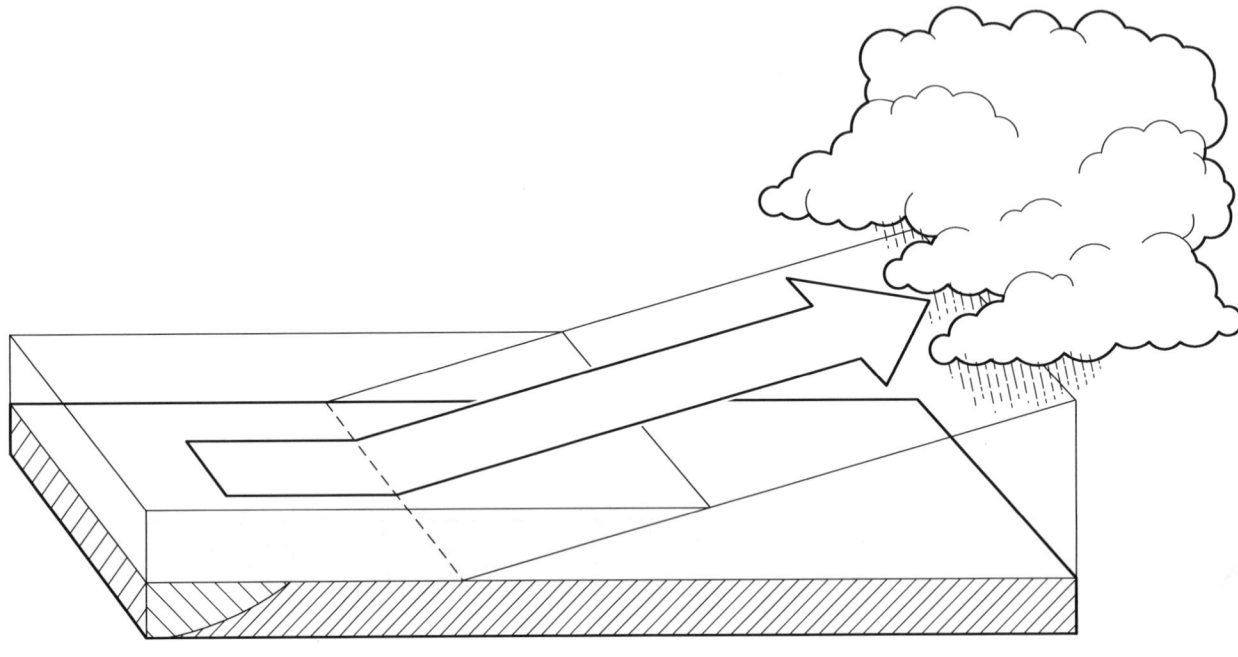

2 Number the following statements to show how this type of rainfall takes place.

Rising air cools.

Warmer, lighter air rises over heavier, colder air.

Warm air meets cold air.

Precipitation takes place.

Condensation occurs and clouds form.

Forecasting the weather – anticyclones

Anticyclones are areas of high pressure.
They usually bring fine, dry weather and
are most common in summer.

An anticyclone in summer

Risk of thunderstorms at end
of 'heat wave' conditions
bringing heavy rain and risk of
flooding.

Very little cloud.

No rain.

Light winds.

Cool nights.

The sun is strong.

Drought in places.

Little rain in some places.

Early morning dew and mist.

Settled weather for days.

Hot, sunny days.

Sun high in the sky.

An anticyclone in winter

Puddles may freeze over.

Light winds.

Very little cloud.

Sun low in sky.

Water pipes may burst
and homes flooded.

Very cold nights.

Days can be clear and bright.

Any fog may last all day.

Early morning frost.

No rain.

Cold days.

Settled weather for days.

 Study the two spider diagrams.

 ◆ Colour red any boxes that are the same
in summer and winter.

 ◆ Colour green the boxes that are different
in summer and winter.

 In your book or file, give reasons for the
similarities and differences between
anticyclones in summer and winter.

❸ It's the summer holidays and high pressure!
You're off camping in Cornwall. List **five**
things you'll pack to cope with the weather.

 ◆ _____

 ◆ _____

 ◆ _____

 ◆ _____

 _____

Summer and winter anticyclones

   Complete the Venn diagram below using the labels in the word box.
Words or phrases that relate to summer and winter anticyclones
should be written where the two circles overlap.

**Summer
anticyclone**

**Winter
anticyclone**

Hot, sunny days	Heat wave	Cool nights
Light winds	No rain	
Very little cloud	Settled weather for days	Cold days
Very cold nights	Frost and fog	

2   Choose three of the labels and explain why you have located them in
a particular place in the Venn diagam.

Label: _____

_____

_____

Label: _____

_____

_____

Label: _____

_____

_____

Forecasting the weather – depressions

Depressions are low pressure areas and bring stormy winds, cloud and rain. They are the most common weather systems affecting the British Isles.

The diagram below shows a depression over London on Saturday 5 April at 3:45 pm, half time for the football matches at the five grounds.

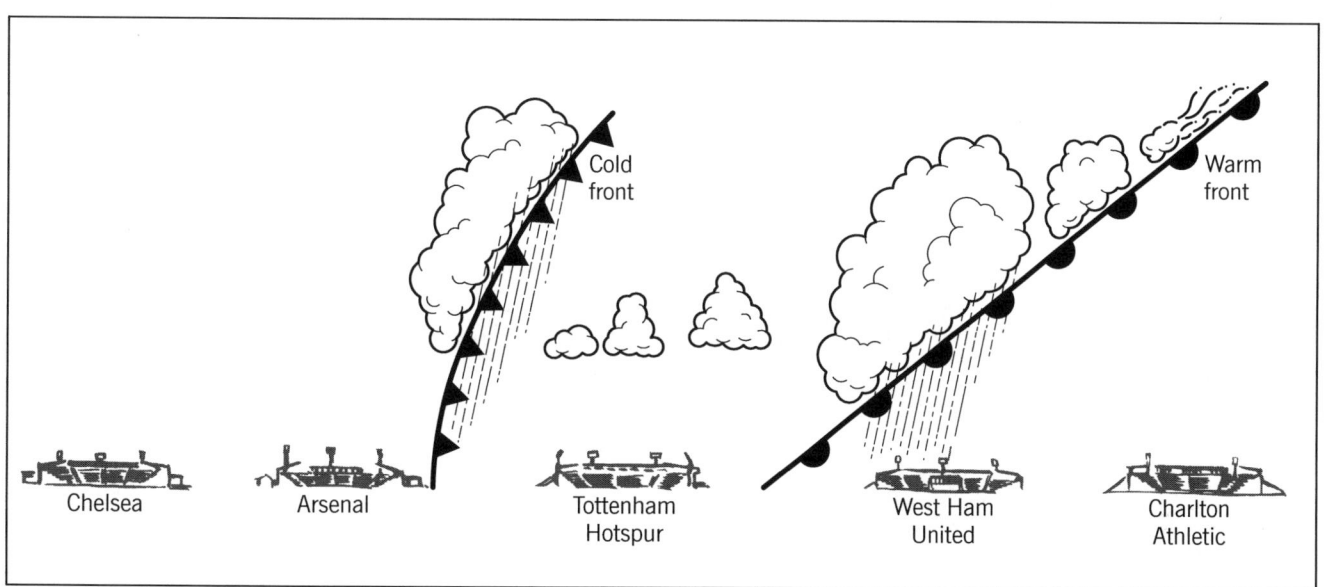

 1   Study the diagram above to find out which team each person below supports.

It is quite cold but very sunny. I can see only a few small clouds high in the sky. I thought the weather forecast was rain! I support
_____.

It is cold but at least it has stopped raining and the sky is clearing. I got very wet walking here from the car park. I support
_____.

It is quite warm and dry now with only a few clouds in the sky. But it was cloudy during the first half. Time to put away the brolly. I support
_____.

It is cold and wet now, but it was warm and cloudy when I arrived at the football stadium. I wish I'd brought my coat! I support
_____.

It got windy and started drizzling just before kick-off. It rained all during the first half and now I am very wet and very cold! I support
_____.

 2   It is 7 am on Saturday 5 April. There is a cold front approaching London. Write the weather forecast for a local radio station.

The passage of a depression

Using the three synoptic charts below, complete the table to show how the weather in Bristol will change as the depression passes over. Circle the correct answers in each row of the table.

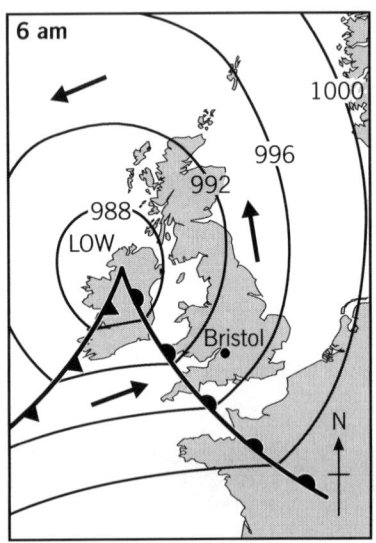
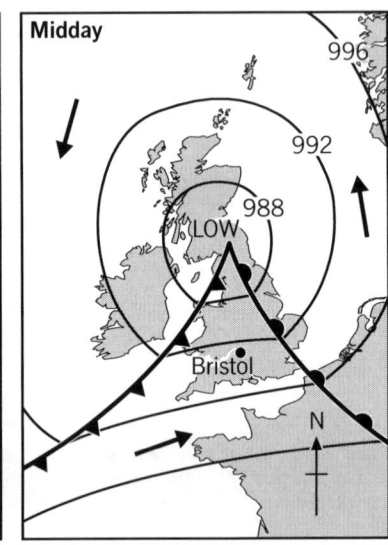
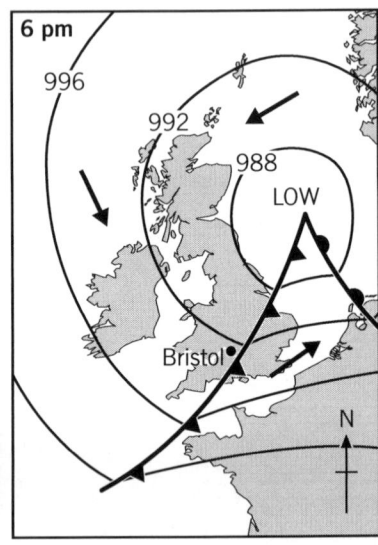

Bristol	6 am	Midday	6 pm
Temperature	Temperature increasing	Temperature increasing	Temperature increasing
	Cold	Cold	Cold
	Warm	Warm	Warm
Precipitation	Dry	Dry	Dry
	Light drizzle	Light drizzle	Light drizzle
	Heavy rain	Heavy rain	Heavy rain
Cloud cover	Clear skies	Clear skies	Clear skies
	Light cloud	Light cloud	Light cloud
	Heavy cloud	Heavy cloud	Heavy cloud
Wind speed	Light breeze	Light breeze	Light breeze
	Calm	Calm	Calm
	Fresh gale	Fresh gale	Fresh gale
Air pressure	Rising	Rising	Rising
	Falling	Falling	Falling
	Unchanged	Unchanged	Unchanged

Weather and climate dominoes

 a Cut out the dominoes below and on Activity Sheet 2.21b and
study the key words written on them.

b Working in pairs, lay all the dominoes in a straight line.

c Now arrange the dominoes in the correct order. You may
only put a domino in place if you can explain to your partner
the link between the words that you are putting together.
There is only one correct order!

START	Winds blow in a clockwise direction

Depression	Where warm air rises gently over colder air

Weather	Violent weather system found in the Tropics

Monsoon	Winds blow in an anticlockwise direction

Convectional rainfal	Lines of equal pressure shown on a weather map

Air mass	FINISH

Anticyclone	Weather system found in SE Asia

Hurricane	Violent weather system over land

Weather and climate dominoes

Frontal rainfall	Air showing similar temperature and moisture features

Rainfall caused when air is forced to rise and cool over upland areas	Climate

Average weather conditions	Where cold air rapidly undercuts warm air

Tornado	Relief rainfall

Isobars	Day-to-day changes in the atmosphere

 Stick the dominoes in your book or file in the correct order.

The weather enquiry

Section 1 | The Introduction

Student   Assessor

Have you:

- included an aim ☐ ☐
- defined the terms weather and climate ☐ ☐
- included an annotated map that shows the regional pattern of weather in Britain ☐ ☐
- described the regional pattern of British weather ☐ ☐
- described the different weather conditions found in the four climatic regions of Britain ☐ ☐
- used facts and figures that highlight these differences? ☐ ☐

Section 2

To succeed make sure you:

- present accurate data in the table on page 38 ☐ ☐
- carry out detailed research to find accurate information on weather and climate ☐ ☐
- colour code the table on page 38 to show patterns in the weather (hottest, wettest, coldest, driest) ☐ ☐
- complete the tables for each family ☐ ☐
- calculate the total points for each location to see which one suits best. ☐ ☐

Section 3

In your reply to the World Wide Leisure Corporation, include:

- four recommendations that match each family to a location in Britain ☐ ☐
- reasons stating why this is the best location for each family ☐ ☐
- specific facts and figures from the tables on page 39. ☐ ☐

Extension

To really develop your answer:

- justify why the other sites were not suitable for each family. ☐ ☐

Think about your learning!

Before you submit your final enquiry, spend some time thinking about the learning that you have carried out.

1 Look carefully at this list of skills. Geographers are skilled people! **Tick** the skills you are developing during your time working on this enquiry.

2 Describe **one** thing that enabled you to be successful in this task:

_____

_____

_____

_____

_____

3 Describe **one** problem you had, or thought you had, that stopped you from achieving your potential:

_____

_____

_____

_____

_____

Teamwork	☐
Reading	☐
Listening	☐
Discussion	☐
Problem solving	☐
Decision making	☐
Map interpretation	☐
Graphing	☐
Data analysis	☐
Questioning	☐
Debating	☐
Time management	☐
Presenting	☐
Empathy	☐
Annotation	☐
Evaluation	☐
Research	☐
Using ICT	☐
Comparing	☐

4 In these boxes write **two** actions that you will carry out to help you be more successful and reach your target in the future.

_____

_____

_____

_____

_____

_____

_____

_____

_____

𝟑 River flooding

KEY IDEAS:

- ◆ the water cycle
- ◆ what happens to rain when it reaches the ground
- ◆ the causes of flooding and how we respond

- ◆ contrasting the effects of flooding in Britain and Bangladesh
- ◆ reducing the risk of flooding.

PoS	Key questions	Pupil book	Suggested activities/methods
6c ii	Why is flooding a problem?	40, 41	Discuss with pupils their perceptions of the effects of a major flood upon their home area.
6d ii	How does the water cycle work?	42, 43	Explain the water cycle. Describe effects on steep/gentle slopes and on tarmac, grass, soil and sand. Describe river formation.
6c i	What is a river basin? Where are the world's most important rivers?	44, 45	Define source, channel, tributaries and mouth. Rivers flow into the lakes/sea. Use of crossword and map to identify and locate world rivers.
6c ii	What causes a river to flood?	46, 47	Examine the reasons for river floods in terms of increased, or faster, inputs of water to the system. Explain how human activities can affect inputs through urbanisation and deforestation.
6c ii	How did floods affect people in southern England in October 2000?	48, 49	Discuss the causes, and consider which are major and which are minor. Develop the idea that they are interrelated. Write a newspaper report on the floods, using key technical terms in their correct context.
6c ii	How does the UK cope with floods?	50, 51	Discuss the different strategies that people in the UK adopt to cope with floods. Phone or e-mail Floodline to find out more information about their work.
6c ii	How did the floods affect people in Bangladesh in 2004?	52, 53	Examine the causes of the floods and compare them with the UK. Examine the effects and compare them with the UK.
6c ii	How did Bangladesh cope with the floods? How and why do responses to disasters in an LEDC differ from those in an MEDC?	54, 55	Examine Bangladesh's strategies for dealing with floods. Compare them with those in the UK. Discuss why Bangladesh has a more extreme problem than the UK does.
6c ii	How can flood risks be reduced?	56, 57	Each method of flood reduction can be examined to see whether it reduces inputs, slows down inputs, stores them until danger has passed or speeds up their removal. Consider the strengths and weaknesses of each method.
1	How can the enquiry process be used to decide how a valley should be protected from flooding?	58, 59	Pupils undertake a geographical enquiry to decide how best to protect the Doveton valley from flooding.

PoS	Skills
1	Undertake a geographical enquiry
2c	Find more information in an atlas using the index
2d	Interpret aerial photos
2d	Interpret satellite photos
4a, 4b	Explain stream flow on a hydrograph

Vocabulary and technical terms

(see Glossary in pupil book)

Condensation	Groundwater	River mouth	Transpiration
Deforestation	Precipitation	River source	Tributary
Evaporation	Reservoir	Stores	Urbanisation
Flash floods	River basin	Surface water	Water cycle
Flood	River channel	Transfers	Watershed

Assessment for Learning

Pupils should swap sheets and mark each other's work. As well as indicating where they are correct, they should explain why incorrect answers are incorrect.

Differentiation

Tick two incorrect boxes to give pupils a starting point. Tell them how many other incorrect answers they are looking for.

Extension

Ask pupils to colour code the corrected boxes to show inputs, outputs, stores, flows and processes.

Pages 44–45: Activity Sheet 3.6

Remove the words from the word box. As a class, draw up the words to go into the word box before they begin the activity. Pupils should explain why each word is important as they suggest them.

Differentiation

Less-able pupils could complete the exercise by using a storyboard and producing a diagram for each stage of the journey rather than producing a written description.

Extension

Ask pupils to predict how Danny Droplet's journey would be different if he landed: a) on a leaf; b) on the division between two drainage basins; c) straight into the river channel; d) on saturated ground; e) on ground covered in snow.

Pages 46–47: Activity Sheet 3.8

In pairs, pupils draw up a list of the factors that will affect the flood risk in the village. Pupils should justify to each other why each factor would increase the risk of flooding in this case.

Differentiation

Provide a writing frame for pupils by outlining which factors affect flooding in this case.

Extension

Ask pupils to think of developments to the village that, in future, would increase the risk of flooding.

Pages 48–49: Activity Sheets 3.11a and b

Once the ranking exercise is complete, draw up a list of success criteria on the board. This can be used to help answer Activity 1 on page 49 of the pupil book more successfully.

Differentiation

Reduce the number of reports to two.

Extension

Pupils should underline the sentences they consider to be the ones that gain marks and explain in writing what it is about each sentence that makes it a success.

Pages 50–51: Activity Sheet 3.15

Pupils should complete this activity sheet in pairs. They should justify their choice of location to each other. Using a whole class question and answer session, ask pupils to justify the location of particular statements and ask others to explain why the statement cannot go in another area of the graph.

Differentiation

Reduce the number of statements or annotate the graph to signify where the statements should go before photocopying.

Extension

Pupils should think of another three labels of their own.

Pages 52–53

To ensure that pupils produce detailed and accurate answers to Activities 2 and 3 on page 53 of the pupil book, they should be introduced to the PEE model. This provides them with a framework for their answers. P stands for Point – pupils should say what their answer is. E stands for Evidence – pupils should produce a fact to back up their point. E stands for Explain – pupils should describe the link between their Point and the Evidence. This model improves the quality of pupils' explanations significantly.

Pages 54–55: Activity Sheet 3.20

Each pair of pupils should add one of the strengths or weaknesses to a master copy of the activity sheet at the front of the class. Once the activity is complete, the master copy can be shown to the rest of the class who can judge the success of their own efforts by seeing how many of the overall strengths and weaknesses they had thought of.

Differentiation

Give pupils a list of strengths and weaknesses that they can choose from.

Extension

For the weaknesses, pupils could make recommendations as to how the Flood Action Plan could be improved.

Pages 56–57: Activity Sheet 3.23

Once the diagram is annotated, pupils should return to pages 56–57 of the pupil book to assess what they have achieved. Using a different coloured pen, pupils add in the missing labels. This could be carried out on their own work or by swapping books with another classmate.

Differentiation

Pupils name each flood prevention scheme and label one advantage of each flood prevention scheme.

Extension

Pupils could add a person who would be for or against each particular kind of flood prevention scheme. These people are detailed in Activity 3 on page 57 of the pupil book.

Pages 58–59: The river flooding enquiry

The river flooding enquiry Checklist (page 96) can be used:

a   by pupils to check whether or not they have fulfilled all of the tasks for the enquiry. Once they think they have finished the enquiry, they can read through the Checklist ticking the parts they have completed. If there are any parts not ticked, pupils can be sure of what they need to include to complete the enquiry.

b   by an assessor (either a teacher or another pupil if an element of peer marking is to be introduced) to mark pupils' work. Once again, the boxes that remain empty will diagnose where the pupil has failed to meet the criteria. The work could be returned to the pupil once an assessor has looked at the work so that any omissions can be corrected by the pupil. This process of drafting work is an important skill for geographers.

The Think about your learning! assessment sheet (page 97) allows pupils to reflect on the work they have undertaken during the enquiry. By considering how they approached a task, pupils can compile a list of their own success criteria and analyse barriers to their learning. This information will better prepare them for the next enquiry.

Why is flooding a problem?

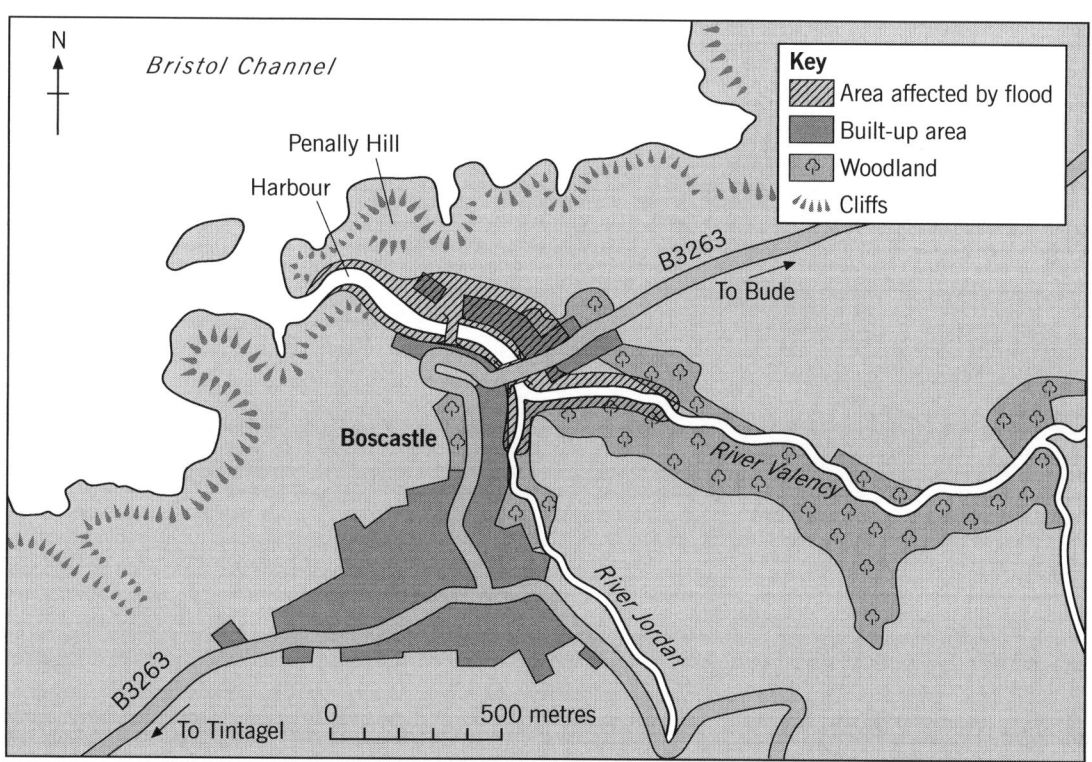

Floods can cause much damage and seriously affect people's lives. There are usually several different causes of floods but some places are more at risk than others.

 Study the events listed below. Each event took place in Boscastle, Cornwall during the flood of 16 August 2004.

Truro and Plymouth hospitals put on standby in case of casualties.	Helicopters start returning to base.	Flood carries boulders, trees and telegraph poles.
	Floods start to recede.	
River flow in Valency and tributaries begins to increase.	Extreme rainfall begins to fall in parts of north Cornwall.	3 metre wall of flood water sweeps across car park; deep fast-flowing water makes the B3263 impassable.
Holidaymakers sit sheltering from the rain in their cars in Boscastle car park when it starts to rain.	Floods at their peak; cars washed down from car park.	First of seven helicopters from Royal Navy, RAF and Coastguard on scene.
	Cornwall Fire Service gets first call for help.	
Valency begins to spill over north bank between the two bridges.		Valency at Boscastle almost full after three hours of extreme rainfall.
Local coastguard warns Falmouth Coastguard of incident developing at Boscastle.	Main road bridge blocked by debris, causing water levels upstream to rise rapidly.	Fire Service and Coastguard declare a major incident.
	At the height of the floods, rescue helicopters begin winching people from buildings.	Fire crews from five Cornish towns sent to Boscastle in next hour.
Water levels on car park rise and cars start to be carried through village by flood water.		Cars in car park start to float; water on B3263 a few inches deep.
	Water levels back within riverbanks.	

 The timeline on Activity Sheet 3.1b can be used to show the events in Boscastle around the time of the flood. Cut out each event above and place each against the most suitable time on the timeline.

Why is flooding a problem?

9 pm

8 pm

7 pm

6 pm

5 pm

4 pm

3 pm

2 pm

1 pm

12 noon

Facing a flood – you decide

There is no easy way to cope with floods. For this activity, you will need to 'think' yourself into the situation of a family facing a flood.

A   **Imagine that you live in Boscastle, Cornwall.** Your Mum works from home. Your Dad is a farm worker. You have one brother and one sister. You hear on the radio that your area is about to be hit by floods with water that will come high up the walls of your home.

Your family can save five things from the flood water. What will you save? Where will you go? How do you feel?

_____

_____

_____

_____

_____

B   **The floods have swamped Boscastle.** Police in a boat rescued you when the floods came and you have spent the last two days and nights in the local village hall. Your brother has a temperature.

It is two days after the floods came. What do you have to eat and drink? What is it like at night? Did you save the right things? What are you and your parents doing? How do you feel?

_____

_____

_____

_____

C   **Two weeks later the floods have gone.** You have gone back to your home. The floors are thick with filth brought by the floods.

What could you do next time to be more prepared? Who or what will help you prepare? What do you need in order to prepare?

_____

_____

_____

_____

_____

How does the water cycle work?

Water can be stored in the sea, in the air and on land. The water cycle is the never-ending transfer of this water between the sea, the air and the land.

 a Each of the statements below shows one part of the water cycle.

b Working with a partner, cut out all the cards and place them, in the correct order, on the water cycle diagram on Activity Sheet 3.3b.

c When you are confident that all labels are in the correct place, carefully glue them down.

Rain that falls onto the ground will soak into the soil and rocks or flow over the surface.	These clouds are moved towards the land by the wind.	The water in the seas and oceans is again evaporated so the cycle begins once more.	As the rain falls towards the earth's surface, some of it is caught by plants and vegetation.
Water on the surface runs downhill as surface run-off and eventually flows as streams and rivers.	The sun's energy heats any water surface like seas and oceans, and causes the water to evaporate.	The hot air containing this water vapour rises and cools down.	This water later evaporates back into the atmosphere by transpiration.
Clouds rise over the land and this causes rain.	The streams and rivers run down slopes to the seas and oceans.	Underground water slowly moves towards the seas and oceans or appears on the surface again as a spring.	As it cools, the water vapour condenses to form clouds.

How does the water cycle work?

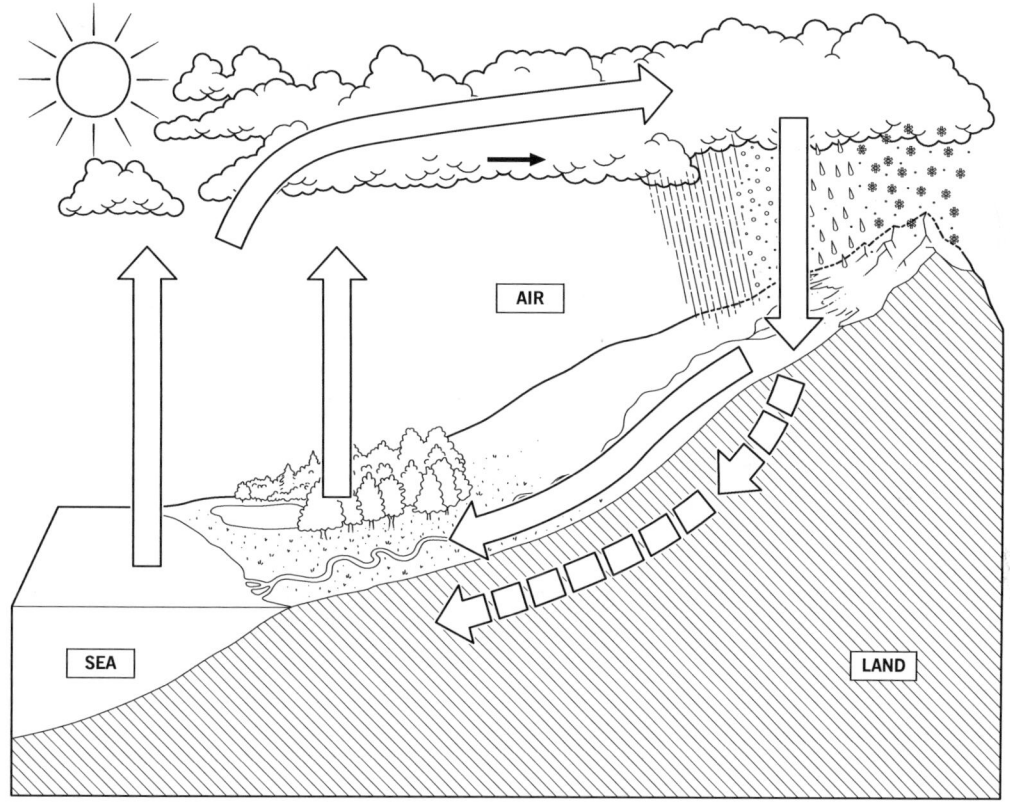

 Colour the arrow on the diagram:

◆ **red** if the sun powers the movement of water

◆ **blue** if the movement of water is powered by gravity.

The water cycle

The diagram below shows the water cycle. It is incorrect as some of the labels have been mixed up. Annotate the diagram by ticking the labels which are correct and crossing the labels that are incorrect. For each incorrect label, write an explanation in the table below of why it is wrong.

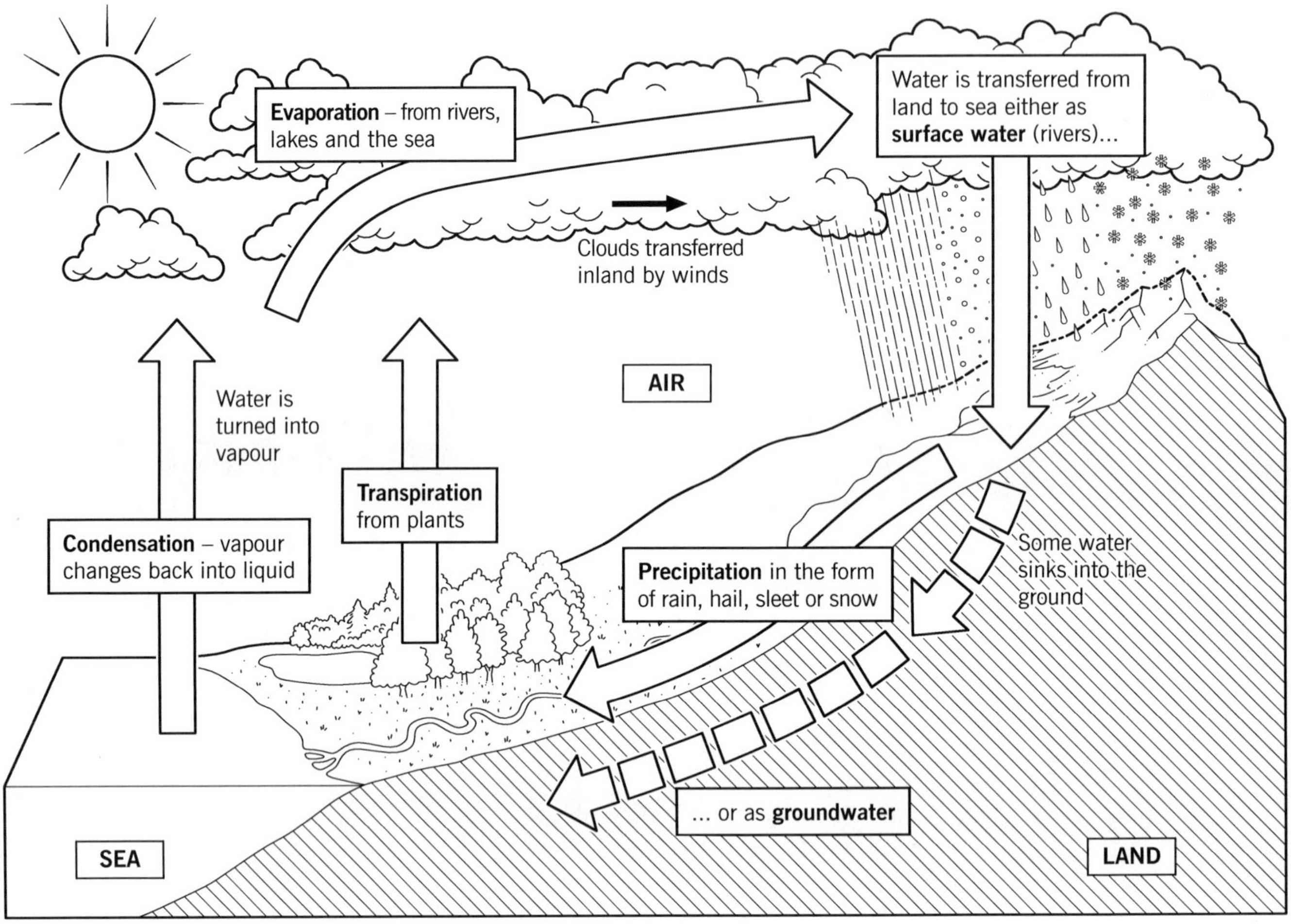

Evaporation – from rivers, lakes and the sea

Water is transferred from land to sea either as **surface water** (rivers)...

Clouds transferred inland by winds

AIR

Water is turned into vapour

Transpiration from plants

Condensation – vapour changes back into liquid

Precipitation in the form of rain, hail, sleet or snow

Some water sinks into the ground

... or as **groundwater**

SEA

LAND

Incorrect label	Why is it wrong?

What is a river basin?

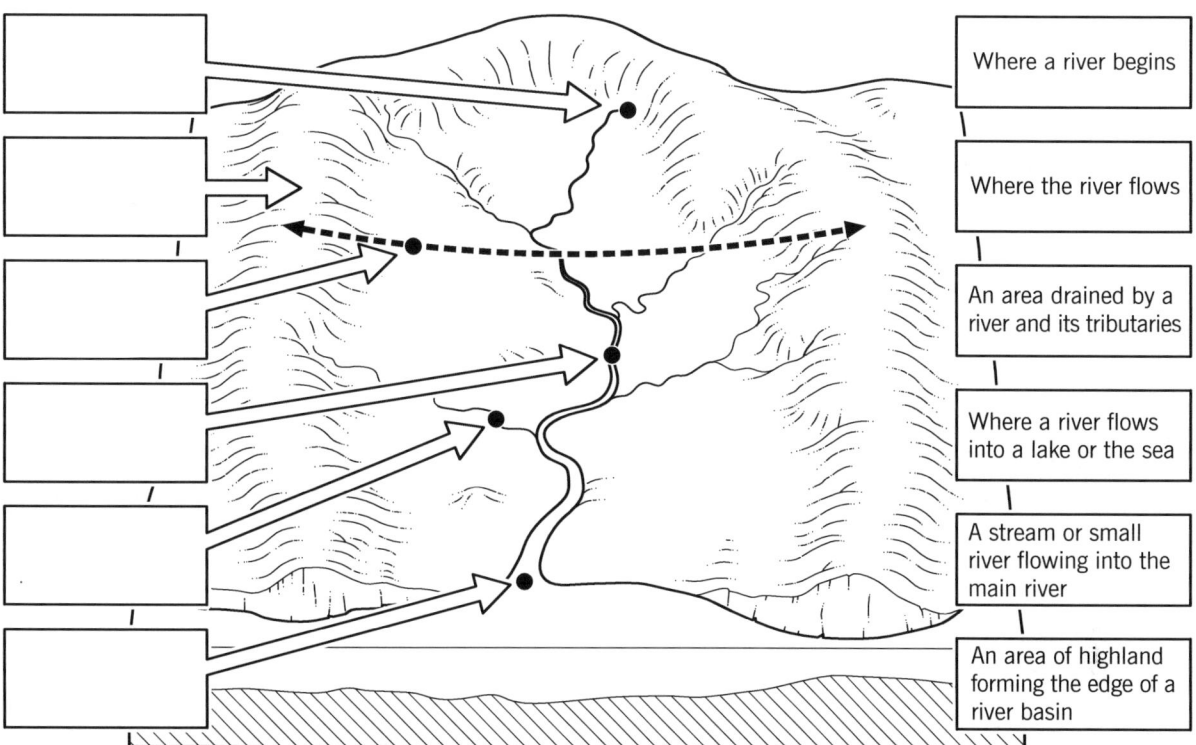

Where a river begins

Where the river flows

An area drained by a river and its tributaries

Where a river flows into a lake or the sea

A stream or small river flowing into the main river

An area of highland forming the edge of a river basin

Rain collects in rivers in a river basin. Rivers have their sources in highland areas and flow in a channel to the sea or a lake.

 Study the sketch that shows the features of a river basin.

 Complete the sketch by writing the letters of the statements in the list opposite in the correct place.

A A river begins at its source.
B The boundary or edge of a river basin is called a watershed. It is usually on high ground.
C A drainage basin is in an area of land where rain collects.
D Rivers flow in a channel. The channel has riverbanks and a riverbed.
E Rivers flow into the sea or a lake. The end of a river is called the mouth.
F A tributary is a small river. Tributaries flow into a main river.

❸ Below is a completed crossword about the features of a river basin. Write the across and down clues. It has been started for you.

Across

1 _____

6 _____

7 _____

8 _____

Down

2 _____

3 _____

4 <u>Where a small river joins a larger one.</u>

5 _____

Crossword grid:

- 4 down: C O N F L U E N C E
- 1 across: M O U T H
- 2 down: T R I B U T A R Y
- 3 down: S O U R C E
- 5 down: W A T E R S H E D
- 6 across: D R A I N A G E B A S I N
- 7 across: S E A
- 8 across: C H A N N E L

Danny the rain droplet

During a rain shower, Danny Droplet has fallen from the clouds and landed just inside the watershed of Figure **B** on page 44 in the pupil book.

Describe Danny's journey through the drainage basin from the source of the river to its mouth.

Try to use all of the words in the word box on the right in your written description.

Watershed	Source	River basin
Tributary	Channel	Mouth

What causes a river to flood?

River flooding is most likely after heavy rain or rapid snow melt. The flood risk is greatest when water is unable to soak into the ground. Human activities can increase the chance of flooding.

Below is a list of words to do with river basins and flooding.

1	Sand.	13	Urbanisation.	25	Precipitation.
2	Tarmac.	14	Evaporation.	26	Channel.
3	Concrete.	15	Condensation.	27	Source.
4	Dam building.	16	Drainage basin.	28	Watershed.
5	Planting trees.	17	Surface water.	29	Stores.
6	Gutters and drains.	18	Groundwater.	30	Lake.
7	High tides.	19	Typhoons.	31	Few trees.
8	Roots.	20	Grass.	32	Impermeable rock.
9	Snow melt.	21	Raising river banks.	33	Hurricanes.
10	Vegetation.	22	Tidal waves.	34	Monsoons.
11	Tributary.	23	Underground drainage.	35	Floods.
12	Deforestation.	24	Heavy rain.		

 a Working with a partner, study the sets of numbers below, which match to words in the list above.

   b Cross out the 'odd one out' in each set.

   c Add a fourth number to match the other two.

   d Explain what links the three 'in' numbers.

Set A	1	2	3	
What's the link?				
Set B	19	33	20	
What's the link?				
Set C	24	35	4	
What's the link?				
Set D	5	9	21	
What's the link?				
Set E	27	6	23	
What's the link?				
Set F	22	14	35	
What's the link?				

What is the flood risk to the village?

Look at the diagram below. It shows the location of a village that may be at risk of flooding. Write a brief report explaining what the flood risk to the village is. Explain which factors affect flooding and why.

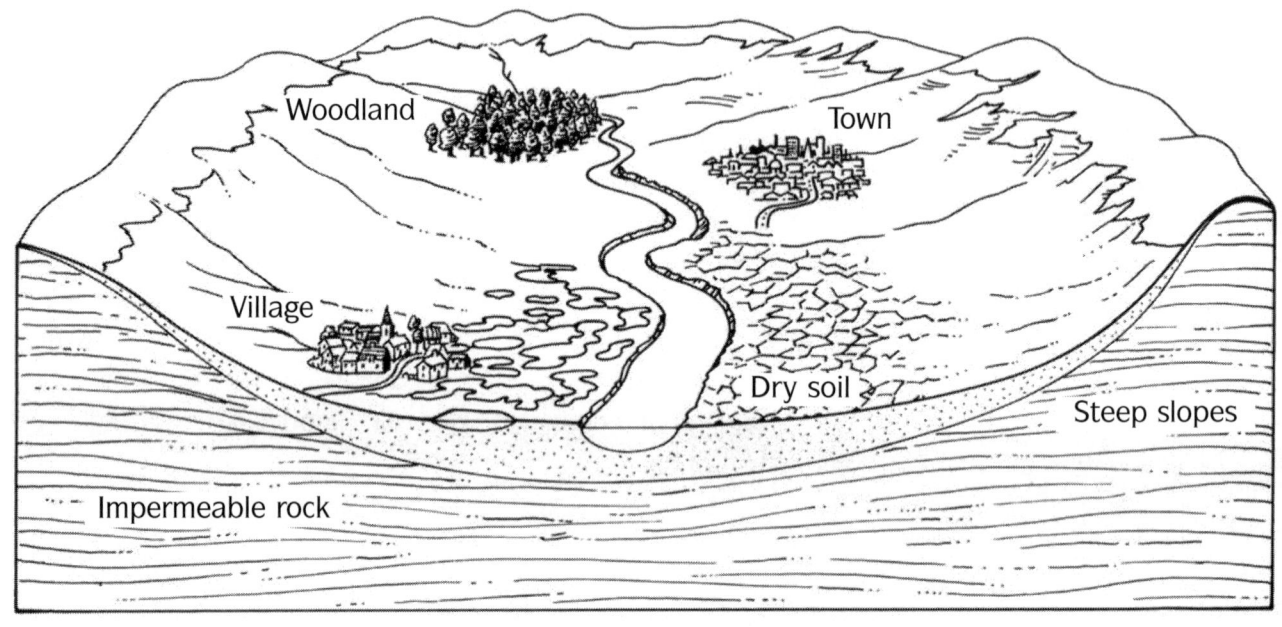

_____

_____

_____

_____

_____

_____

_____

_____

_____

_____

_____

_____

_____

_____

Floods in the UK, 2000

River flooding is most likely after heavy rain or rapid snow melt. The flood risk is greatest when water is unable to soak into the ground. Human activities can increase the chance of flooding.

1 Read statements **A–I** describing the causes and the effects of floods in the UK.

2 Write each statement's letter into the flow diagram in an order which makes sense to you.

A More than a month's rain fell in 24 hours.

B The ground became full of water and could take no more.

C Rain falling on concrete or tarmac is unable to soak into the ground, so stays on the surface.

D The Met Office says that autumn 2000 was the wettest since records began in 1776.

E In some parts of the country, water levels were at their highest for 100 years.

F In the south of England much of the land is low lying.

G Torrential downpours and storms caused rivers to burst their banks and water flooded surrounding areas.

H Heavy rain had been falling in the area for more than a week.

I Recent building in floodplain areas made the problem worse.

3 Use the information above and on pages 48 and 49 in the pupil book to write a paragraph explaining what caused the floods in the UK in 2000.

Packing an emergency supply flood kit

People living in high-risk flooding areas are advised to keep an emergency supply kit packed, ready and stored in case a disaster strikes. For this activity, you will need to 'think' yourself into the situation of a person facing a flood.

 Below is a list of items that may be part of this emergency supply flood kit. Suggest reasons why each item should be included. It has been started for you.

 Highlight essential items in **red** and the useful items in **green**.

Item	Reason for inclusion
Toilet paper and bucket with lid.	Drains will not work in a flood.
Candles.	
Emergency numbers to ring.	
Family medication.	
Gas and water keys.	
First-aid kit and medication.	
Important papers and cash.	
Torch, spare bulbs and batteries.	
Flashlight, battery-powered radio and spare batteries.	
Bottled water (3 days' supply) and purification tablets.	
Emergency tinned food and tin opener.	
Blankets.	
Snack foods high in water and sugar.	
Camping stove, matches and gas.	
Picnic hamper with plastic cutlery.	
Sleeping bags.	
Extra warm clothes.	
Spare shoes.	
Waterproof heavy-duty plastic.	
Toiletries and personal hygiene items.	
Comfort items like games, crayons and paper.	
Money.	
Non-electric kettle.	
Wellington boots.	

 Working with a partner, add any further items to the list you would include in your own emergency supply flood kit. Give reasons why each item should be included.

 What precious possessions would you try to rescue? Explain why.

Flood disaster report

Look at the three reports below and on Activity Sheet 3.11b. They were written by pupils as responses to Activity 1 on page 49 in the pupil book.

One report is a poor answer, one is average and the other is good.

Read through the reports and decide which is the good one, the average one and the poor one. Give reasons for your decision.

Flood disaster Report 1
Sunday 14 October 2000

Last week the worst floods in 30 years hit the county of Sussex in Southern England. A number of settlements in East Sussex were badly hit including the towns of Uckfield, Haywards Heath, Lewes and Etchingham.

The damage caused by the flooding has been widespread. Thousands of homes were flooded including 300 homes in Lewes. People have been left homeless and have lost all of their personal belongings. Local businesses have been badly affected; shops and offices have been flooded and their contents damaged. A brewery in Lewes flooded and the racecourse in Brighton had to cancel a meeting because the racecourse was under water.

Rail travellers were badly affected in Haywards Heath because services were disrupted by the flooding. This caused a problem for commuters who were not able to get to work. Car owners have also been affected because most of the roads in the region have been blocked, including the A26 and A22 where some motorists were trapped in several feet of water.

Flood victims have been offered help; people have been evacuated from homes and cars by people like the Coastguard and Fire Brigade. People who have been left homeless have been provided with refuge in a local school and church by the Council. The Government has also promised flood victims support.

The river levels are dropping but have left behind many problems. A thick, foul-smelling mud has been left behind and will take weeks to clean up. People who are homeless may not return to their houses for weeks. Businesses that were flooded have lost money whilst they were shut and they will have to pay for the stock that was lost in the flood. Insurance companies will have to pay out an estimated £500 million pounds in compensation.

In conclusion, the floods in East Sussex have been devastating for people and businesses alike and the clean up could take months.

Flood disaster report

Flood disaster Report 2
Sunday 14 October 2000

Last week the UK's worst floods hit the county of Sussex in Southern England. A number of settlements in East Sussex were badly hit.

The damage caused by the flooding has been widespread. Homes were flooded and people have been left homeless. Shops and offices were flooded.

Rail travellers were badly affected. Car owners were also affected, roads were shut.

Flood victims have been offered help by the Coastguard, Fire Brigade, Council and Government.

The river left behind mud and will take weeks to clean up. People are homeless. Insurance companies will lose a lot of money when they have to pay people compensation.

Flood disaster Report 3
Sunday 14 October 2000

The damage caused by the flooding has been widespread. Many homes were flooded and people have been left homeless. Shops and offices were flooded including a brewery in Lewes and the racecourse in Brighton.

Flood victims have been offered help; people have been evacuated from homes and cars by people like the Coastguard and Fire Brigade. People who have been left homeless have been provided with refuge in a local school and church by the Council. The Government has also promised flood victims support. Rail travellers were badly affected in Haywards Heath because services were disrupted by the flooding. This caused a big problem for commuters who were not able to get to work.

The river levels have dropped and left many problems. A thick, foul-smelling mud has been left behind and will take weeks to clean up. People who are homeless may not return to their houses for weeks. Businesses that were flooded have lost money whilst they were shut and they will have to pay for the stock that was lost in the flood. Insurance companies will have to pay out an estimated £500 million pounds in compensation.

How does the UK cope with floods?

The Environment Agency is an organisation that looks after rivers in England and Wales. If flooding is forecast, the Environment Agency's Floodline issues warnings. It also gives advice on what to do before, during and after a flood.

 1 Number the following advice within each of the three sections in an order of priority that makes sense to you.

Before a flood

____ **Move** your car to higher ground.

____ **Check** on nearby neighbours.

____ **Seal** all your rubbish and any chemicals.

____ **Collect** warm clothes, food and a torch.

____ **Ring** Floodline for information – Tel: 0845 988 1188.

____ **Listen** to warnings on the TV and local radio.

____ **Block** doorways and airbricks with sandbags.

____ **Switch-off** electricity and gas.

____ **Move** people, pets and valuables to safety.

____ **Raise** valuable furniture.

____ **Be alert** for flood warnings and take action.

____ **Tie** and roll up your curtains if you can.

____ **Know** where your family is.

____ **Get** your flood kit ready.

During a flood

____ **Never** walk, drive or swim through flood water.

____ **Listen** to the local radio for flood news.

____ **Avoid** flood water as it may be contaminated.

After a flood

____ **Throw** out contaminated food.

____ **Check** if it is safe to turn electricity and gas on.

____ **Open** windows and doors for ventilation.

____ **Beware** of rogue traders offering to help.

____ **Call** your insurance company for advice.

____ **Wash** taps and run them before use.

____ **Clear** up by disinfecting walls and floors.

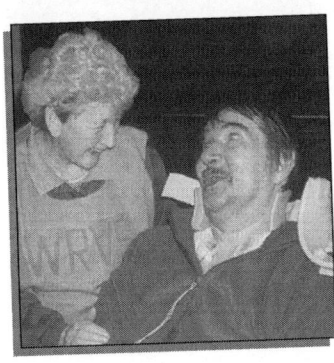

2 **a** Imagine that your neighbourhood gets flooded to the depth of a school ruler – that's 30 cm! Use this measure to guess the water level inside and outside your home.

b Make a list of all the damage and problems that would be caused by the flood water.

c If the flooding lasted for a week, what further problems would be created for you and your family? Add these to your list and compare with a partner.

Be prepared for floods

Design a 'Be prepared for floods' poster using statements from the list below. Add your own artwork.

- Know how to turn off gas and electricity.
- Check your neighbours.
- Tie and roll up your curtains if you can.
- Raise valuable furniture.
- Seal all your rubbish and any chemicals.
- Listen to warnings on the TV and local radio.
- Don't drive through flood water.
- Get your flood kit ready.

- Don't touch items that have been in contact with the water. It is likely to be contaminated and could contain sewage.
- Move your car to higher ground.
- Know where your family is.
- Ring Floodline for information – Tel: 0845 988 1188.
- Get sandbags.

How does the UK cope with floods?

Floods can cause much damage and seriously affect people's lives. The statements below show people and organisations that respond to flooding.

1 Working with a partner, study the statements. Decide whether the people and organisations respond before, during or after a flood. Colour the statements as follows:

- ◆ Colour the first circle red if they respond **before** a flood.
- ◆ Colour the second circle yellow if they respond **during** a flood.
- ◆ Colour the third circle green if they respond **after** a flood.

Be careful! You may need all three colours for some statements.

Ambulance service takes the injured, cold, wet or those in a state of shock to hospital.
Before   During   After

Plumbers repair water supplies in people's homes.
Before   During   After

Local people look after families, friends and neighbours.
Before   During   After

Water Board provides clean, safe drinking water and treats household waste/sewage.
Before   During   After

Electricians make power supplies safe and repair faulty wiring in people's homes.
Before   During   After

Fire and rescue service provides trained people with specialised equipment.
Before   During   After

Meteorological Office provides weather forecasts and weather warnings.
Before   During   After

Police Force helps people to safety and stops looters entering empty homes.
Before   During   After

Borough Council is responsible for local planning like emergency shelter and sandbags.
Before   During   After

Army and Air Force provide trained people with specialised equipment.
Before   During   After

Local radio and newspapers have regular weather forecasts, flood warnings and up-to-date advice and information across each region.
Before   During   After

Insurance companies consider flood damage, check claims and pay out money to people who have insurance policies.
Before   During   After

Environment Agency provides warnings and defences against the threat of flooding.
Before   During   After

2 Add two further groups of people and organisations that respond in times of emergency. Colour each one to show how each responds to floods.

Before   During   After

Before   During   After

How does the UK cope with floods?

Floods can cause much damage and seriously affect people's lives.

Each of the statements on Activity Sheet 3.14a shows people or organisations that can help in times of floods.

 3 Working with a partner, decide which type of organisation each is and, using the words in **bold**, complete the table below by ticking the correct columns.

 4 Add two further people or organisations that can help in times of floods.

	Respond **before** a flood	Respond **during** a flood	Respond **after** a flood
Rescue and emergency services.			
Organisations that provide warnings and try to prevent flooding.			
Organisations that give help and advice.			
Businesses that provide a service to homeowners.			
Organisations that provide emergency planning.			
Volunteers.			

 5 Imagine that your class has been asked to write a flood plan for your neighbourhood. Your plan should contain three sections. How to:

   ◆ stop floods and flood damage from happening

   ◆ warn people when a flood may happen

   ◆ respond to the emergency when a flood has happened.

Don't forget to use the information about people and organisations that can help before, during and after a flood in your plan.

A flood episode

Look at the graph below. It shows the height of a river during a flood episode. In pairs, read through the statements underneath the graph. You need to write the number of each statement in the correct place on the graph. Number 1 has been done for you.

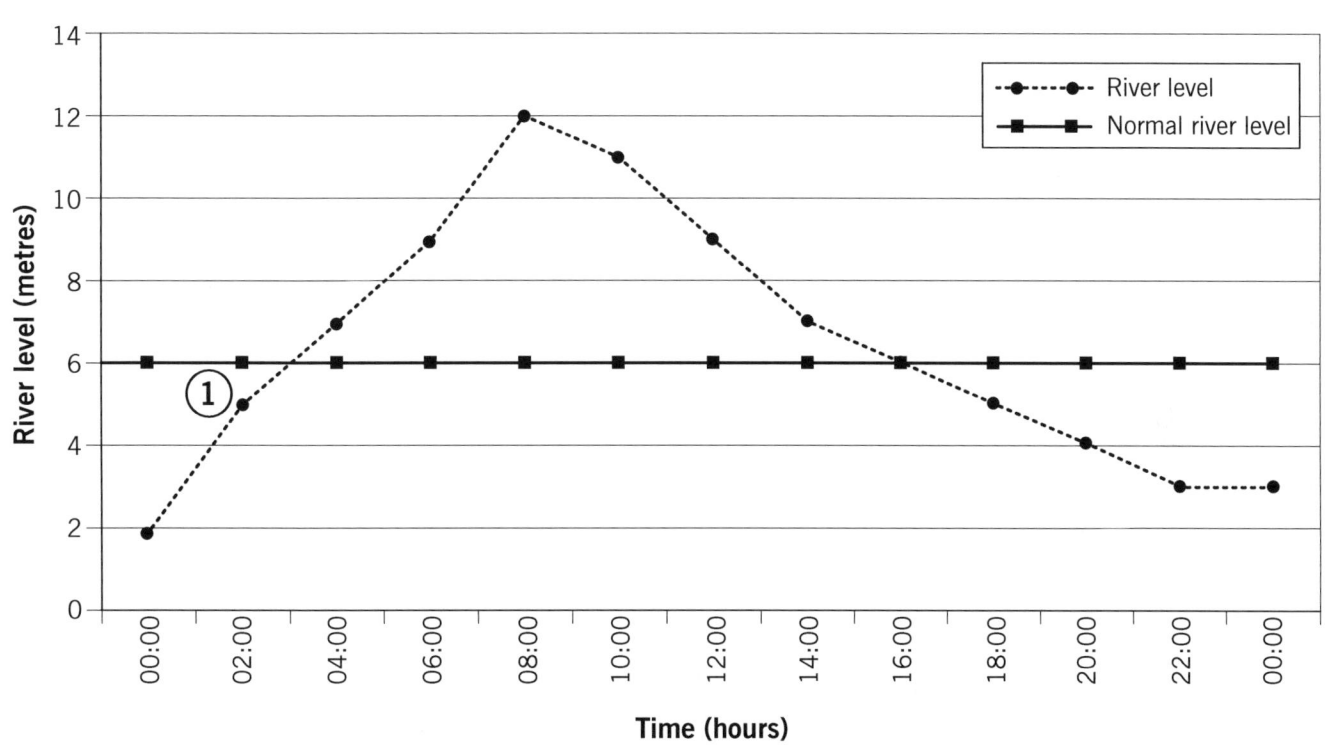

Time (hours)

---

1 Check on family and neighbours.

2 Collect warm clothes, food and a torch.

3 Switch-off electricity and gas.

4 Listen to the local radio for flood news.

5 Never walk, drive or swim through flood water.

6 Avoid flood water as it may be contaminated.

7 Throw out contaminated food.

8 Wash taps and run them before use.

9 Call your insurance company for advice.

10  Flood Watch

11 Severe Flood Warning

12 All Clear

Floods in Bangladesh, 2004 – asking questions

Floods can cause much damage and seriously affect people's lives. There are usually several different causes of floods but some places are more at risk from flooding than others.

Imagine that you are a newspaper reporter assigned to report on the flood disaster. On your way to the flood you must plan your research.

What was the damage?

Where did it happen?

When did it happen?

Who was affected?

Why did it happen?

How were the people affected?

1 Working with a partner or in a small group, study the photo and questions above.

2 Think of more questions to help you find out what is happening and help the newspaper's readers to understand the disaster. Write these questions in the boxes. Your questions should begin with: What? Where? Who? When? Why? How?

What caused the floods in Bangladesh, 2004?

The floods of 2004 were very severe but serious floods are common in Bangladesh. Much of the country floods on a regular basis. Floods may result from natural events or from human activity. Bangladesh has floods nearly every year because the River Ganges overflows its banks.

1 Read the following 14 statements describing the causes and the effects of floods in Bangladesh.

2 Write each statement's letter into the flow diagram below in an order that makes sense to you.

A The Himalayas and Bangladesh get very heavy monsoon rain.	**G** Both river flooding and tidal storm surge linked to cyclones happen in late summer.
B Huge rivers quickly bring the water towards Bangladesh.	**H** Tropical cyclones often occur with river floods caused by monsoons.
C Rivers are most likely to flood because of deforestation in the Himalayan foothills.	**I** Cyclones bring high waves, storm surges and heavy rainfall.
D On reaching Bangladesh, the rivers easily overflow their banks.	**J** Buildings, bridges and crops are destroyed.
E Flooding is most likely in late summer after heavy monsoon rains and snow melt in the Himalayas.	**K** Not enough to eat as crops have been destroyed.
F Tropical cyclones are most likely to happen in late summer and early autumn.	**L** Heavy rain for many days.
	M Levels of the rivers rise.
	N The ground becomes full of water and can take no more.

3 Using the information above and on pages 52 and 53 in the pupil book, write a paragraph explaining what caused the floods in Bangladesh in 2004.

Floods in Bangladesh, 2004

1 **a** Cut out the dominoes below and study the key words written on them.

b Working in pairs, lay all the dominoes in a straight line.

c Now arrange the dominoes in the correct order. You may only put a domino in place if you can explain to your partner the link between the words that you are putting together. There is only one correct order!

START	Bangladesh

When a river overflows its banks	Dysentery

Cutting down trees	Urbanisation

More built-up areas	Monsoon rain

A country found in Asia	Himalayas

Mountain range north of Bangladesh	Dhaka

Roads and railways under water	Rice crop destroyed by floods

Disease spreads during floods	Transport links destroyed

Extended period of heavy rain	River delta

Capital city of Bangladesh	Deforestation

Area of flat land where a river meets the ocean	Flooding

People starve	FINISH

2 Stick the dominoes in your book or file in the correct order.

How does Bangladesh cope with floods?

Poor countries like Bangladesh find it very difficult to cope with floods. The effects of flooding are therefore a lot worse than they would be for a rich country.

> The floods came very suddenly. Everybody was taken by surprise. We have been sheltering on the corrugated iron roof of our flooded home for days. I have lost two of my oldest children to the flood. They were just washed away in the night and never seen again. We have lost our homes, lost our land and lost our cattle. Our crops have been ruined and we have no food or money. Without help we will starve.

 In a group, discuss the life of the mother, her family and neighbours. You should consider:

- ◆ the heavy monsoon rains that continue to fall

- ◆ people left homeless

- ◆ the spread of diseases

- ◆ crops ruined by the flood water

- ◆ the risk of starvation

- ◆ roads and railways that have been swept away.

2 Write a paragraph continuing the story of the mother and her fight for survival.

_____

_____

_____

_____

_____

_____

_____

_____

_____

_____

_____

How successful is the Bangladesh Flood Action Plan?

In pairs, think back over what you have learned about preventing flooding in Bangladesh. Use the diagram below to organise your thoughts. Annotate the scales with bullet points to evaluate how effective the Bangladesh Flood Action Plan has been.

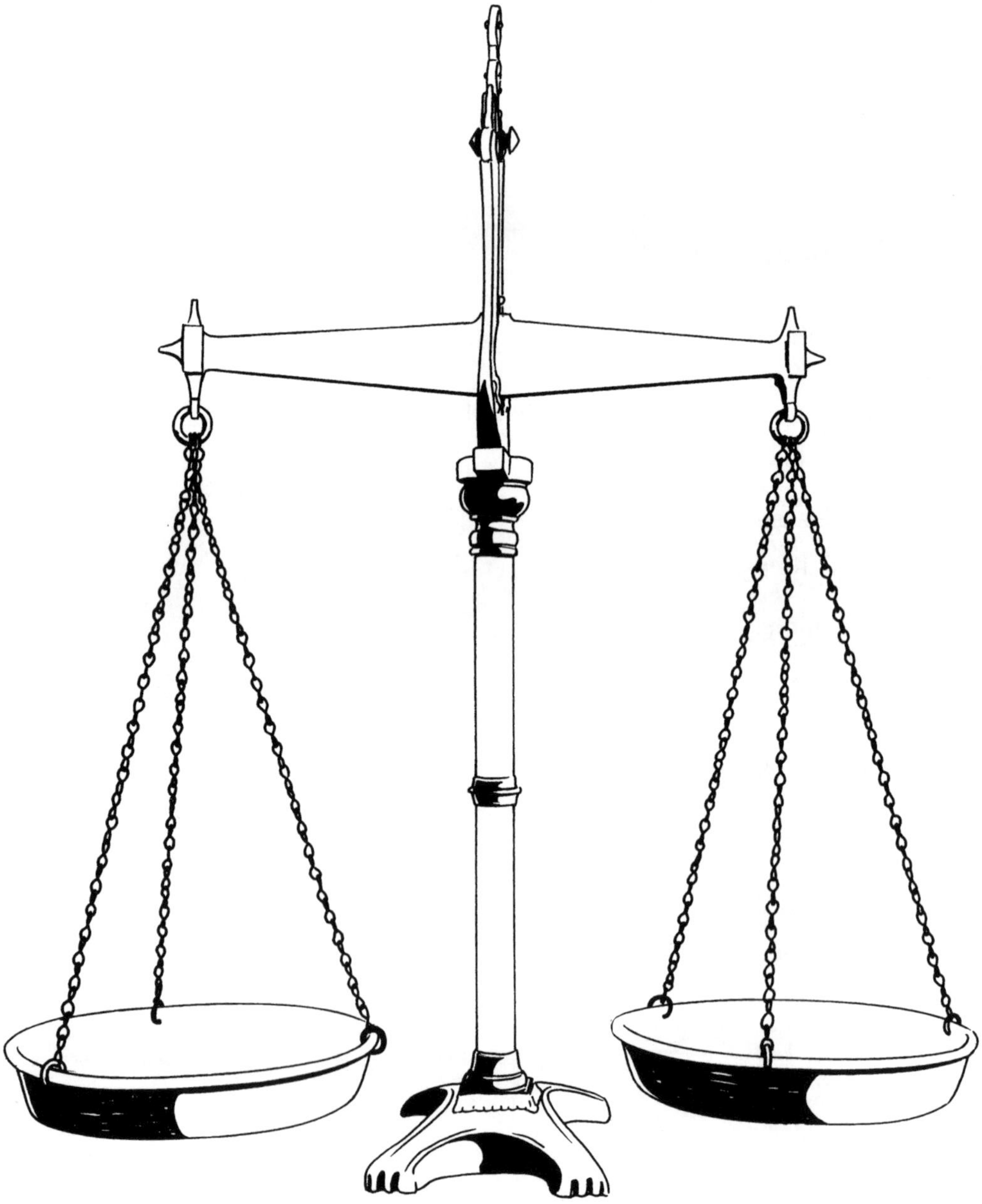

How can the risk of flooding be reduced?

Imagine that the Bangladeshi government planned to build a dam on the River Brahmaputra in the north of the country to control flow and hold back the monsoon rainwater in reservoirs.

 Read the questions below and work out where each question fits around the development compass.

 Write the questions in one of the four spaces around an enlarged copy of the development compass.

- ◆ Will people have any say in the decision about the dam?
- ◆ How much will the dam cost?
- ◆ How many families will be forced to move?
- ◆ Will it provide jobs?
- ◆ How many towns and small villages will be lost forever?
- ◆ Will the dam affect people further down the river?
- ◆ How will the Bangladeshi people benefit from the dam?
- ◆ Will it lead to a loss of fertile silt to land downstream?
- ◆ How much land will be submerged?
- ◆ Will people be paid any compensation for moving?

- ◆ How will people feel about having to move?
- ◆ Will flood damage be reduced and lives saved?
- ◆ How will the dam affect fish and threaten wildlife?
- ◆ Who will make the final decision about the dam?
- ◆ Will land for resettlement be on higher land with thin, infertile soils?
- ◆ Who will make money from building the dam?
- ◆ How will the Bangladeshi economy benefit from the dam?
- ◆ Will Bangladesh have to borrow money to pay for the dam?

Nature and the environment

Who decides and choices for possible futures

Economic and trade issues

Social issues and the people

 Add two further questions to the development compass.

How can the risk of UK flooding be reduced?

A variety of methods can be used to reduce the risk of floods, but there is no way to stop flooding. A modern approach is to allow parts of a river to flood naturally.

1 Read what people say about flood prevention schemes below.

A Flooding is a natural event. It has always happened. In the past, people were sensible enough to live well away from rivers and floodplains. It's their own fault if people are having problems with flooding.

G The lives and property of people are much more important than what the countryside looks like. I blame the county council for not keeping up with river defences to stop these floods. I want to know how they are spending all the money I pay in business rates and taxes.

B Don't people understand why the flat land next to rivers is called a floodplain? If people live somewhere that is prone to flooding – it's their own fault. I say let flooding happen!

F I think that recent floods are a result of global warming. More government money could lead to better prevention measures but, even then, we cannot remove the risk of flooding when all's said and done.

C Building new houses on flat land is much easier than building on slopes! Buying floodplain land from farmers is cheap because it can only be used as summer pasture for cattle. I think we're making better use of floodplain land.

D We must use all the ways possible to stop flooding – using all the modern technology we have. If this means concrete walls and flood barriers, so be it!

E I bought this new house for over £300,000 last summer. Last winter, after heavy rain, the local river flooded my house not once, but twice! I wonder what it's worth now?

2 Which people think that river flooding can be stopped? On the line below, put the letters **A** to **G** where you think they should go.

Impossible to stop flooding		Flooding can be stopped by spending lots of money

3 Place an 'X' on the line above to show your own opinion. Explain your answer.

4 Why do you think different people have different opinions about river flooding and how to stop it?

What are the advantages and disadvantages of flood prevention schemes?

There are eight examples of flood prevention schemes below. Your task is to complete the information boxes.

You *must* add the name of the flood prevention scheme and one advantage.

You *should* add one disadvantage for each flood prevention scheme.

You *could* add the name of a person who would be in favour of using each type of flood prevention scheme.

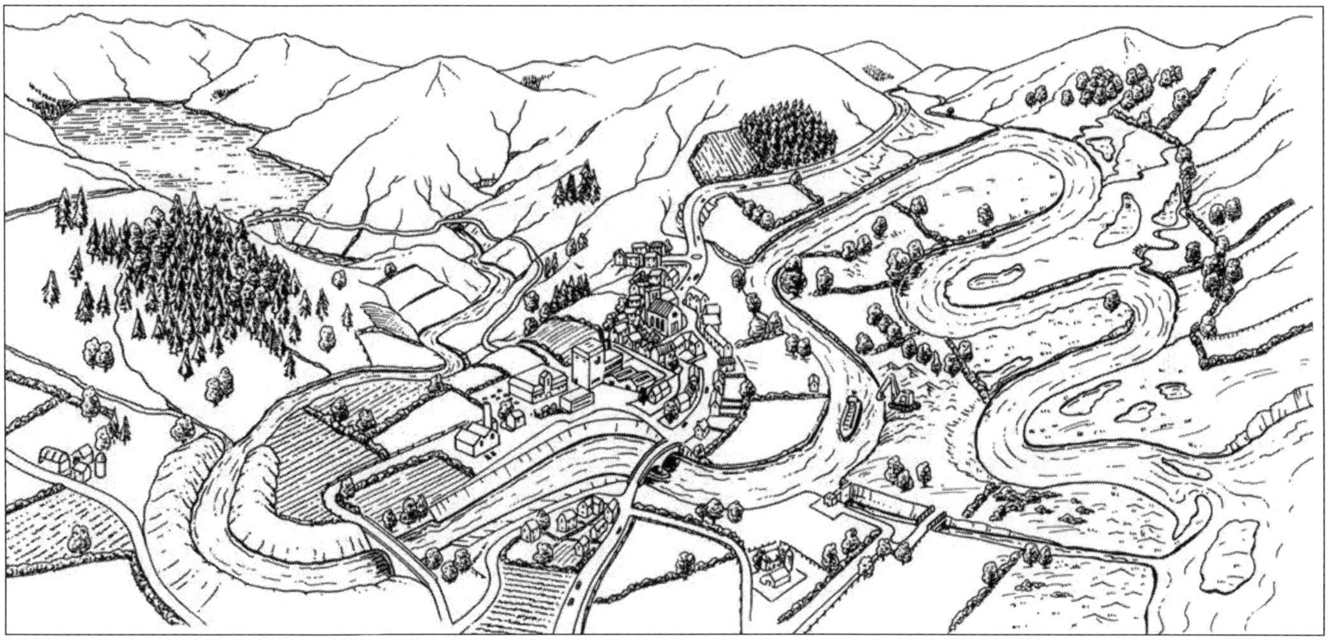

1

2

3

4

5

6

7

8

Comparing floods in the UK and in Bangladesh

Poor countries like Bangladesh find it very difficult to cope with floods. The effects of flooding are therefore a lot worse than they would be for a rich country.

Use the Venn diagram below to compare the problems faced by flood victims in the UK with those in Bangladesh.

 a Study the factors in the following list.

b Place the letters of the factors in the Venn diagram to show which factors are most likely to affect which victims.

c Any effects that are shared by both countries should be written where the two circles overlap.

A	No safe drinking water.	**N**	Families separated.
B	Electricity cut-off.	**O**	International aid sent from abroad.
C	Starvation.	**P**	Evacuation plans.
D	Emergency services rescue people.	**Q**	Insurance cover.
E	Homeless people.	**R**	Buildings and property damaged.
F	Roads impassable.	**S**	Animals drowned.
G	Food and shelter for the homeless.	**T**	Rail services cancelled.
H	Medical care.	**U**	Sewage contaminates water supplies.
I	Government help.	**V**	Clean-up operation.
J	Crops destroyed.	**W**	Flood warnings.
K	Spread of disease.	**X**	Homes destroyed.
L	People dead.	**Y**	Water Authority pumps water away.
M	Lost belongings.	**Z**	People stranded on rooftops.

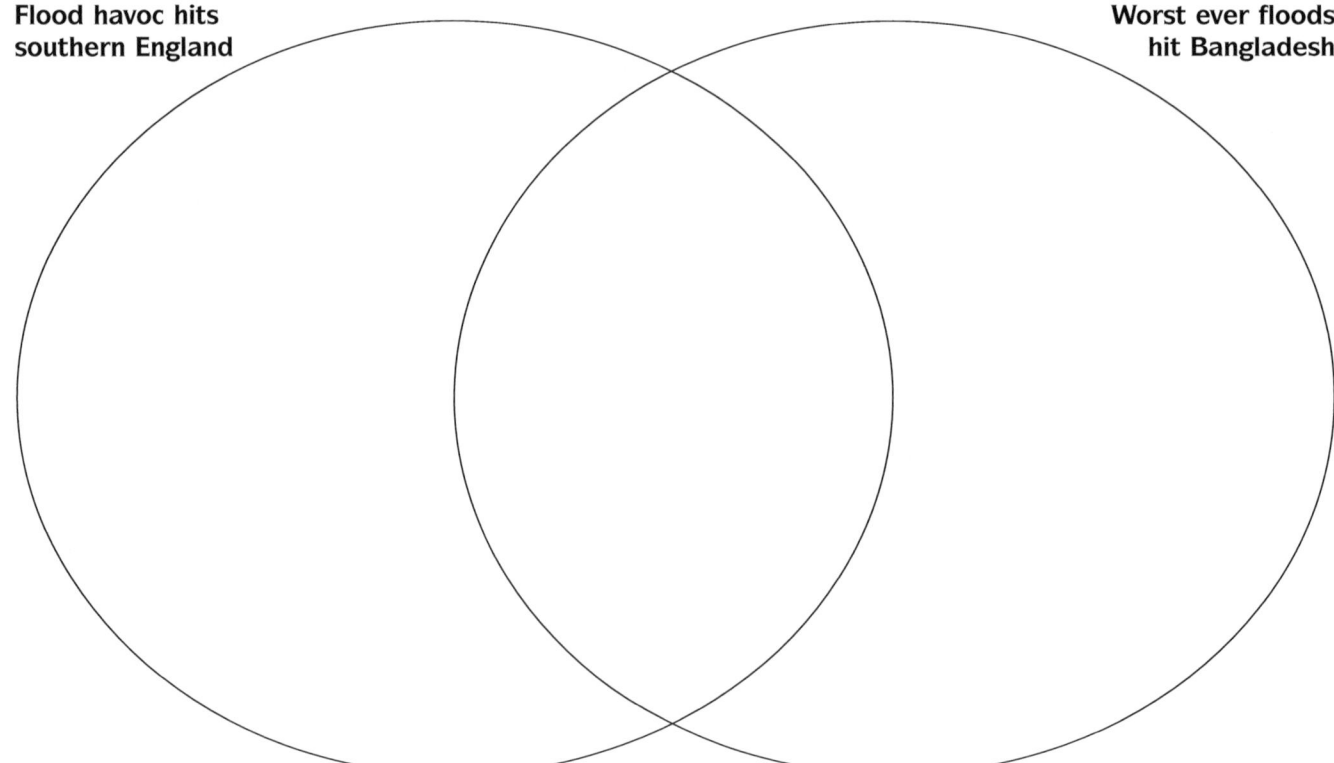

Flood havoc hits southern England

Worst ever floods hit Bangladesh

 For any five statements, explain the damage caused by flooding.

 'Flood victims in Bangladesh suffer more than flood victims in the UK.' Do you agree with this statement? Explain your answer.

Comparing floods in the UK and in Bangladesh

Use all you have learned about floods to describe the similarities and the differences between the causes and effects of flooding in the UK and in Bangladesh. You may find this writing frame useful to structure your work.

Sentence starters

I have been studying...   If we compare...   In [date]...

Flooding in the UK and Bangladesh has had many effects. In many ways the two floods had different effects. These effects included...

_____

_____

_____

_____

_____

_____

Linking words

although   but   whilst   in contrast   however   whereas   then
this caused   and so   because of this

There were also several similarities in the two floods. These were...

_____

_____

_____

_____

_____

_____

_____

_____

Possible endings

Finally   We can see that   Having looked at

In conclusion, I think the floods in _____ had a greater effect than in _____

because _____

_____

_____

_____

The river flooding enquiry

Before you finish your enquiry use the reminders below to make sure that you have covered all of the correct points.

To make a well thought through and effective decision about the best flood protection scheme for the Doveton valley,

you will need to: **Student**   **Assessor**

- make a copy of Table **A** on page 58 in the pupil book ☐ ☐

- read the four scheme descriptions ☐ ☐

- make a list of anything you are not sure about in the four scheme descriptions ☐ ☐

- ask your teacher to explain the points you do not understand ☐ ☐

- evaluate how successful each scheme would be by putting ticks in columns A, B, C or D of your table if the scheme would fulfil that factor ☐ ☐

- add up the number of ticks for each scheme and write in the total score ☐ ☐

- using the total score, make a decision about which scheme you would recommend ☐ ☐

- think about which part of the valley you would like to protect most and then make your decision, if two schemes get the same total scores ☐ ☐

- describe the scheme you would like to recommend ☐ ☐

- justify your decision by explaining the benefits of your scheme for the Doveton valley ☐ ☐

- state whether each of the four characters would be for or against your chosen scheme ☐ ☐

- explain why each character would be for or against each scheme. ☐ ☐

3 River flooding

Think about your learning!

Before you submit your final enquiry, spend some time thinking about the learning that you have carried out.

1 Look carefully at this list of skills. Geographers are skilled people! **Tick** the skills you are developing during your time working on this enquiry.

2 Describe **one** thing that enabled you to be successful in this task:

_____

_____

_____

_____

_____

3 Describe **one** problem you had, or thought you had, that stopped you from achieving your potential:

_____

_____

_____

_____

_____

Teamwork	☐
Reading	☐
Listening	☐
Discussion	☐
Problem solving	☐
Decision making	☐
Map interpretation	☐
Graphing	☐
Data analysis	☐
Questioning	☐
Debating	☐
Time management	☐
Presenting	☐
Empathy	☐
Annotation	☐
Evaluation	☐
Research	☐
Using ICT	☐
Comparing	☐

4 In these boxes write **two** actions that you will carry out to help you be more successful and reach your target in the future.

4 Settlement

Unit Overview

Approximate teaching time, 16 hours

KEY IDEAS:

- how sites for settlements were chosen
- benefits and problems of settlement growth
- land use patterns in towns
- how functions and land use change

- how shopping has changed
- traffic problems and solutions
- how environments may be improved.

Pos	Key questions	Pupil book	Suggested activities/methods
6g i	What are settlements like?	60, 61	Discuss with pupils their image of a typical 'village' and 'city' environment. Discuss why some settlements grow to be larger than others.
6g i, 6g iii	How were early settlement sites chosen?	62, 63	Describe the effect of the environment on the location of early settlements. Decision-making exercise – choose the best site for a settlement. Photo analysis to see the reasons for the site of Warkworth and its site problems today.
6g iv	What different settlement patterns are there?	64, 65	Examine photos to see the main settlement patterns: dispersed; linear; and nucleated. OS map reading to recognise those same patterns in a different area.
6g iii	How has the shape and function of a small settlement changed over time?	66, 67	Study plan of village in the 1890s and 2000s then spot the differences. Role-play the effect of these changes on different members of the community.
6g i, 6g iii	What benefits and problems result from the growth of settlements?	68, 69	Brainstorm the benefits and problems of settlement growth. Does one outweigh the other? Look at the quality of life in urban areas.
6g iv	What patterns of land use can be identified in towns?	70, 71	Define functional zones linked to the sequence of urban development and changes in housing.
6g iv	Why does the land use in towns change and how does this affect groups of people?	72, 73	Use photos to show changes in inner-city areas, e.g. London Docklands. Role-play the effects on different groups of people.
6g ii	Where do we shop?	74, 75	Learn the meaning of 'convenience' and 'comparison' shops and use these terms in context. Carry out a shopping survey. Analyse the results of own, or others', survey.
6g ii	How has shopping changed?	76, 77	Discuss changes in shopping in general, and then see how these changes apply to pupils' own town.
6g ii	What are the impacts of internet shopping?	78, 79	Discuss the advantages and disadvantages of shopping using the internet.
1b, 1c, 1d, 2a, 2b, 2c	Traffic in urban areas – why is it a problem?	80, 81	Study photo, drawing and graph and synthesise information to describe traffic problems in towns. Develop techniques to describe graphs.
4b, 3d	Traffic in urban areas – is there a solution?	82, 83	Study details about alternative solutions and apply them to pupils' own town.
3d, 4b, 2g	Where should the by-pass go?	84, 85	Decision-making exercise on planning a by-pass around a town.
6g ii, 1a–f	Settlement enquiry – how can a city street be improved?	86, 87	Pupils undertake a geographical enquiry to determine how to improve a street in a city.

98

PoS	Skills
1	Geographical enquiry and skills
2c	Map to locate a good position for building
2c	Four figure co-ordinates
2d	Oblique aerial photos
2e	Draw simple sketch map with symbols and a key
2e	Annotated fieldsketch
4b	Describe a distribution pattern thematic map

Vocabulary and technical terms

(see Glossary in pupil book)

Accessibility
By-pass
Central business district (CBD)
Communications
Congestion
Dispersed settlement
Function
High and low order
Inner city
Land use

Linear settlement
Nucleated settlement
Pattern
Public transport
Settlement
Shopping malls
Site
Suburbanised village
Suburbs
Urban model

Assessment for Learning

Pages 62–63: Activity Sheet 4.5

Pupils should work in pairs, justifying their choice of site to each other as they go. As the teacher takes feedback from each pair, pupils should be allowed time to add to or alter their answers. This introduces an element of drafting to pupils' work.

Differentiation
Give pupils a choice of two potential sites for each group. They can choose which one is correct and give reasons why they did not choose the other.

Extension
Ask pupils to choose a second most likely site and explain why it was not the first choice. They should pick out characteristics of the group of people and be linking these characteristics to the natural resources available at the sites.

Pages 66–67: Activity Sheet 4.8

There are a number of Assessment for Learning opportunities throughout this activity. Pupils are asked to design questions to help them fill gaps in their knowledge and understanding of the implications of the changes in the village. They then trade ideas, which means pupils are peer coaching one another. The extension task promotes evaluation of their ideas by listening to other pupils and improving their own thoughts as a result of what they hear.

Differentiation
Reduce the number of changes to be analysed to five. Alternatively, complete parts of the table before the sheet is photocopied to give pupils an idea of how it should be completed.

Extension
Pupils should be posed the following:
◆ Make a list of the factors you need to consider when changing a settlement.
◆ What was the most positive change made to the village and why?
◆ What further changes would you recommend for the village in future?

Once pupils have had time to answer the questions, a whole class debate using people's opinions is a good way for pupils to discover what other pupils think of their ideas and how their ideas could be further improved.

Pages 68–69: Activity Sheets 4.9a and b

Providing success criteria to pupils ensures that they have a clear idea as to what is expected of them. They have a framework around which to formulate their answers.

Differentiation
The success criteria differentiates between pupils of differing abilities. Less-able pupils could be asked to complete only the 'You must...' sections.

Extension
Once pupils have completed their postcard:
◆ ask them to share what they have written with a partner
◆ get the partner to count the number of points the pupil has made in their postcard to Geoff

◆ use pages 68–69 of the pupil book to look back at the problems and benefits of life in a city
◆ the partner writes a list of points the pupil could have made to Geoff along the bottom of the postcard.

Pages 70–71: Activity Sheet 4.11

The mark scheme provided for Activity 2 on page 70 of the pupil book provides pupils with an opportunity to assess the quality of their own work. As well as finding out how well they have done, by adding missing points to their answer they can see what they need to do to achieve greater success. The final two choices (Retired and Your own choice) have been left blank as they are based much more on opinion rather than evidence gleaned from the house adverts. You may wish to conduct a whole class discussion to think of success criteria before pupils begin the activity.

Differentiation
Reduce the number of houses, reduce the number of scenarios or reduce the number of points expected to three.

Extension
Ask pupils to include two paragraphs for three of the families. They must comment on reasons for choosing a house and reasons for not choosing other houses that were for sale.

Pages 72–73: Activity Sheet 4.13

This activity is designed to ensure that pupils think about exactly what information they need to have available to them before they begin question 3 on Activity Sheet 4.12. Planning answers is a fundamental skill but one that we need to train pupils to do. This provides that training. They are assessing their knowledge levels so that they have all of the necessary information to complete the task successfully.

Differentiation
Less-able pupils should be asked to think of fewer economic, social and environmental issues and associated solutions.

Extension
Use high order questions to help students think about different issues and solutions. Question whether the solutions they have thought of are sustainable. This may be a new concept to students but is an important one to introduce to them.

Pages 74–55

The following ideas can be used to extend question 2 on Activity Sheet 4.14.

Choose a pupil to justify the location of one of the statements. Write their answer on the board. Ask other pupils to improve the answer by adding/removing words. Alternatively, ask other pupils to counter argue the first pupil's answer.

Differentiation
Reduce the activity to just characteristics of either a corner shop or shopping centre, or reduce the number of statements.

Extension

Add a third circle to the Venn diagram to include market stalls. Ensure that pupils can justify the location of the statements.

Pages 76–77

There are a number of Assessment for Learning activities that can be carried out before pupils attempt Activities 3 and 4 on page 77 of the pupil book.

Once pupils are aware of the task, they should work in small groups to think of what will make a successful poster/letter in terms of content and presentation. This could be typed and used as a form of self evaluation for the pupils or as a peer assessment tool for other pupils to mark their colleagues' work or for teachers.

Pages 78–79: Activity Sheet 4.18

Activity Sheet 4.18 asks pupils to justify the benefits of internet shopping. By providing pupils with an idea of how many points they need to make to achieve success, they have a clear idea of what sort of end product they are aiming for.

Differentiation

Reduce the number of points expected for each answer for less-able pupils.

Extension

Rather than tell pupils how many points they are expected to make, they should be asked to decide for themselves how many points they think would be necessary to achieve a high level answer.

Pages 80–81: Activity Sheet 4.22

If pupils work in groups to complete the sorting activity, then the discussion they generate will assess the level of understanding that they have of the statements.

Differentiation

Tell the pupils which statements come first and last.

Extension

Classify the statements into social, economic and environmental issues caused by traffic in urban areas.

Pages 82–83: Activity Sheet 4.24

Pupils should work in pairs to share their ideas and help each other to improve their thoughts.

Differentiation

Reduce the number of statements available to the pupils.

Extension

Use differentiated questions as shown in the examples below:

◆ What would be an advantage of building a metro?
◆ Name two schemes that would speed up traffic?
◆ Name a scheme that would improve the safety of an urban area?
◆ Name a management strategy which might appeal to a family/business person?
◆ If you could only afford one scheme, which would it be?

Pages 84–85: Activity Sheet 4.26

The Assessment for Learning aspect of this activity comes from the pupils thinking of their own success criteria before embarking on their presentation. Each presentation is then assessed by one group, which can provide feedback either to the whole class or face to face to the group itself.

Differentiation

Place pupils in mixed-ability groups. Ask higher-ability pupils to take a lead in managing the group and supporting other pupils.

Extension

Once the pupils have presented feedback to other groups, they can swap presentations and use their feedback to improve the quality of that presentation. Introducing a level of drafting is an important skill not exclusively reserved for written work in other subjects!

Pages 86–87: The settlement enquiry

The Checklist (page 131) provides pupils with a framework to attempt the enquiry. This should ensure that they have more structure to their answer, therefore, increasing the chance of success. Once the enquiry is complete, but before it is handed in, pupils can use the self-evaluation column to check if they have included the relevant sections. Teachers can use the final column either to assess the work as it is in progress or once the work is complete. Once completed, the Checklist gives pupils pointers as to which areas they need to improve on in future.

The Think about your learning! assessment sheet (page 132) provides an opportunity for pupils to reflect on the work they have undertaken during the enquiry. By considering how they approached a task, pupils can compile a list of their own success criteria and analyse barriers to their learning. This information will leave them better prepared to approach the enquiry in the following unit.

What are settlements like?

Settlements are places that are useful to people. They provide jobs, shops, offices, entertainment and other services. These are called the functions of a settlement.

 Study the three photos **A**, **B** and **C** on pages 60 and 61 in the pupil book.

 In which photo would the things below be most likely to happen? Enter A, B or C in the left-hand column.

Photo	
	Derelict buildings and disused warehouses.
	Work in a large factory.
	Inner centre redevelopment.
	Have waste land and abandoned buildings.
	Be a bad place for asthma sufferers to live.
	A corner shop open late at night.
	Find people buying and selling goods.
	High-rise flats.
	Find crime, vandalism and litter.
	Empty homes in need of renovation.
	Children playing outside in the street.
	Old buildings being demolished.
	See holiday makers relaxing and enjoying themselves.
	Find an area of factories and old houses next to the city centre.
	See market traders selling fruit and vegetables.
	Find cars speeding.
	Enjoy the 'bright lights' and entertainment.
	Find narrow streets where people still know their neighbours.
	Find boarded-up houses.
	Enjoy parks and open spaces.
	Live in a multicultural society.
	Be stuck in a traffic jam in August.
	Go shopping in new indoor shopping centres.
	Find traffic jams, pollution and noise.
	Find cinemas, clubs, theatres, art galleries and museums.
	Be unemployed.
	Find houses very expensive to buy.

 Choose one of the photos and describe the type of settlement. Remember: Be careful when you are working with different 'points of view'. Your thoughts may be based on labels and unfairness, and not on real knowledge.

What are settlements like?

Most of us live in a settlement of some kind. What settlements are like affects us all in some way or another.

Below is a list of words to do with settlements.

1	Market.	**14**	Greenfield.	**27**	Site.
2	Traffic.	**15**	Port.	**28**	Village.
3	London.	**16**	Congestion charge.	**29**	Pattern.
4	Industrial.	**17**	Linear.	**30**	West Indians.
5	Farming.	**18**	Offices.	**31**	Brownfield.
6	CBD.	**19**	Normans.	**32**	Nucleated.
7	Saxons.	**20**	Resort.	**33**	Norwich.
8	Town.	**21**	Tokyo.	**34**	City.
9	Rome.	**22**	Urban.	**35**	Hamlet.
10	Rural.	**23**	Crowded.	**36**	Apartment.
11	New York.	**24**	Derelict.	**37**	Community.
12	Near water.	**25**	Celts.	**38**	Detached.
13	Suburbs.	**26**	Shops.		

1

a Working with a partner, study the sets of numbers below, which match to words in the list above.

b Cross out the 'odd one out' in each set.

c Add a fifth number to match the other three.

d Explain what links the four 'in' numbers.

Set A	36	3	21	33	
What's the link?					
Set B	10	5	23	35	
What's the link?					
Set C	7	30	19	25	
What's the link?					
Set D	11	3	33	9	
What's the link?					
Set E	23	2	16	3	
What's the link?					
Set F	28	7	8	34	
What's the link?					

How were the sites for early settlements chosen?

Early sites for settlements were chosen because of natural advantages such as good
water supply, dry land, defence, shelter, farmland and building materials.

 In the table below, match each description to its correct factor. Colour the
matching pairs.

	Factor	Order of importance
A south facing slope will have more sun and will be protected from the cold north wind.	Protection.	
Good views from a hilltop give you warning if you are about to be attacked.	Building materials.	
Needed for fires for warmth and to cook on.	Plenty of water.	
Sites must not flood or be marshy.	Shelter.	
Needed wood or stone. Useful to be near a wood or a rocky hillside.	Supply of wood.	
Easier to build on, for growing crops and travelling to other towns.	Rivers.	
Needed for drinking, cooking and washing. Water might come from a river, a spring or a well.	Not too much water.	
Easy to cross either on foot at a ford or by a bridge.	Flat land.	

2 Decide which of these factors would be the most important in choosing a site for a
settlement. Which would be next? Using the right-hand column, number the list of
factors above in order of importance. Explain why you put the factors in this order.

_____

_____

_____

_____

3 Imagine that you are in charge of building a new settlement and have a free
choice over where to build.

  a What factors would be important in choosing the site of a new
settlement in the twenty-first century?

  b How, and why, do you think this would be different from settlements
of hundreds of years ago?

_____

_____

_____

Choosing the best site for a settlement

Early sites for settlements were chosen because of natural advantages such as good water supply, dry land, defence, shelter, farmland and building materials.

 1 Read the statements below. Colour the physical reasons for choosing a site in red and the human factors in green.

> There is a natural harbour.

> Many routes cross or meet here.

> There are good views from a hilltop.

> There is flat, level land for building.

> It is situated above the flood level of a river.

> There is good farmland with fertile soils.

> There is a gap in the hills.

> There is access to a good water supply.

> There is a spring nearby.

> It is near a river.

> A mine and quarry are nearby.

> It is sheltered from storms.

> It is on the sunny side of a valley.

> There is a wood nearby.

> It lies at the bridging point of a river.

 2 Decide which of these factors would be the most important in choosing a site for a settlement. Which would be next? In your book or file, list the statements above in order of importance. Explain why you put the factors in this order.

 3 Can you think of any situations where the order of importance might change? Explain your answer.

Which group of people is most likely to live here?

Using Figure **B** on page 62 in the pupil book, complete the table below.
Match each group of people to an appropriate site (**A–E**). Each site
should be used, two sites will be used twice. Once you have matched
the groups of people to their sites, justify your choice.

Group of people	Site chosen	Justification
Roman soldiers		
Potters		
Cattle farmers		
Basket weavers		
Market gardeners		
Wood carver		
Sheep farmer		

What different settlement patterns are there?

Geography is about people and places. It helps us to understand our world and makes it a more interesting place in which to live. You are connected to people and places all over the world in a variety of ways.

Your task is to investigate a place you know well – your local town or city. Produce a written report with photos, maps and diagrams.

Resources: TV, video, CD-ROMs, magazines, books, the internet, Tourist Information can all provide words and pictures to help you. You may like to use the framework below to help structure your work.

1 What is it?
Is it a village, town, a suburb, a city borough?

Is it an industrial town, a market town, a regional centre, a port, a holiday resort?

2 Where is it?
Describe its location using an atlas.

Can you give an Ordnance Survey grid reference?

Is it on a hill, by the coast or inland?

Draw a labelled sketch map to show the location.

3 What is it like?
Describe the landscape – physical and human features.

Is the place busy/quiet, large/small?

Describe its industries and jobs.

Describe its transport links like road and rail.

4 How did it get like this?
What is its history?

What changes have taken place?

Has the place grown?

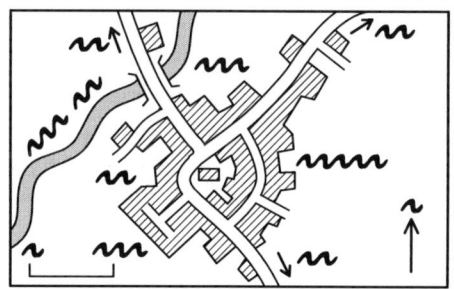

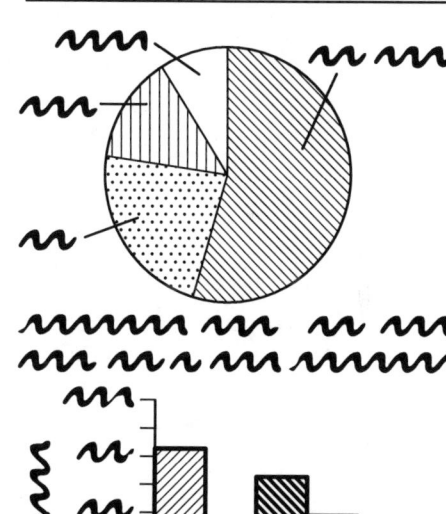

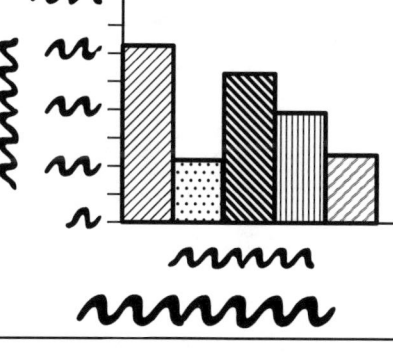

5 How is it changing?
Are people moving in or moving out?

Are there fewer or more jobs?

6 Extra
What might happen in the future?

How is it linked to other places in the UK and the world?

Is it affected by other places and decisions made elsewhere?

How has its importance changed over time?

How do settlements change with time?

 a Cut out the dominoes below and on Activity Sheet 4.7b and study the key words written on them.

b Working in pairs, lay all the dominoes in a straight line.

c Now arrange the dominoes in the correct order. You may only put a domino in place if you can explain to your partner the link between the words that you are putting together. There is only one correct order!

START	A place where people live

SETTLEMENT HIERARCHY	A settlement with normally no services

SITE	The shape of a settlement

OUTER SUBURBS	When a real-life situation is made simple

SETTLEMENT PATTERN	Farms and buildings spread out

INNER CITY	Large detached houses and open space

DISPERSED	Houses are built in a line

FUNCTION	Where people buy and sell things

HAMLET	Everyday goods like bread and milk

How do settlements change with time?

A MODEL	The world's biggest docks in 1926

CONVENIENCE GOODS	Goods not needed very often

MARKET TOWN	Where people make things

LINEAR	High-rise buildings and shops

LONDON DOCKLANDS	They redeveloped the London Docklands

SPECIALIST GOODS	Modern shopping malls on the edge of towns

INDUSTRIAL TOWN	The place where a settlement first grew

CBD	Old industry and terraced houses

LONDON DOCKLANDS DEVELOPMENT CORPORATION	When places are put in order of importance

OUT-OF-TOWN CENTRES	FINISH

SETTLEMENT	The reason why a settlement was built

❷ Stick the dominoes in your book or file in the correct order.

Have changes to settlements been a success?

 Complete a copy of the table below using Figures **A** and **B** on page 66 in the pupil book. For each difference in the village, you need to think of:

◆ why the village has changed

◆ what disadvantage the change may have brought to the village

◆ which groups of people like the change

◆ which groups of people do not like the change

◆ whether you think the change has been successful/ unsuccessful and why.

Do not worry if you are unable to complete all of the table immediately. There will be an opportunity for you to question your classmates to find the missing information later.

Change
1　Building of the by-pass.
2　More car parking at the pub.
3　Farm buildings are converted.
4　A new caravan park has been built.
5　The school has closed.
6　A new old people's home is opened.
7　The village restaurant opens.
8　A craft museum is in the old school.
9　The village pond is drained.
10　The village shop has closed.

	Why has the village changed in this way?	Can you think of a disadvantage of this change?	Who might support this change?	Why might other groups be against this change?	Do you think the change is successful/ unsuccessful? Why?
1					
2					
3					
4					
5					
6					
7					
8					
9					
10					

 Make a list of questions to find out the information that you have not managed to complete so far. For example: 'Who might support the village restaurant opening?'

What are the benefits and problems of settlement growth?

1 Your pen-pal, Geoff, has written to you to let you know that he and his family are moving to London.

Geoff's mother has a new job in London and they have to move next month. He is worried about the big move, he has never lived in a city before, let alone one as big as London.

Your task

Use the postcard template on Activity Sheet 4.9b.

a Write back to Geoff and try and reassure him that there are many advantages to living in a big city.

b Explain to Geoff what is being done to try and make cities like London a great place to live for everyone.

c Once you have finished your postcard to Geoff, decorate the front of the postcard with images/pictures advertising the benefits of life in a big city.

Your success criteria

You must...

◆ give two advantages of life in a city like London.

◆ give two examples of actions that are being taken to try and tackle problems of life in a city like London.

You should...

◆ give at least four advantages of life in a city like London.

◆ give three examples of actions that are being taken to try and tackle problems of life in a city like London.

You could...

◆ carry out some research and give specific examples of the advantages of life in London.

◆ carry out some research and give specific examples of what is being done by London's councils to improve life in London.

What are the benefits and problems of settlement growth?

Mr G Thorne

17 Nelson Avenue

West Millfield

WM12 4UK

What are the different land use patterns in towns?

Land in a town can be used in different ways. Land use depends upon the main function of that part of town.

 1 Look carefully at the four pictures of different types of settlement on Activity Sheet 4.10b.

Picture

_____ Large, modern private houses and council estates.

_____ A bus service into the city.

_____ Old terraced housing.

_____ Home owners gardening at weekends.

_____ The oldest buildings, modern office blocks and shops.

_____ Noisy neighbours.

_____ Derelict buildings and disused warehouses.

_____ Inner centre redevelopment.

_____ A garden centre.

_____ Semi- and detached homes with gardens.

_____ Areas of open space.

_____ Council and private houses.

_____ Schools with good examination results.

_____ New roofs on old houses.

_____ A corner shop open late at night.

_____ Old people and families with young children.

_____ Crowds and busy streets.

_____ Houses built in the 1920s and 1930s.

_____ Vandalism, litter and crime.

_____ Cars parked in garages.

_____ A new supermarket opening soon.

_____ Rows of terraced housing.

_____ Restaurants, cafés, museums, cinemas and entertainment.

_____ High-rise flats.

_____ New shopping centres.

2 In which picture would the features listed below appear? Enter A, B, C or D in the left-hand columns.

Picture

_____ Double-glazing to reduce traffic noise.

_____ Hear football crowds.

_____ Empty homes in need of renovation.

_____ Parking meters.

_____ New, modern industrial estates and business parks.

_____ Pensioners who've lived in the same house all their lives.

_____ Houses with burglar alarms and window locks.

_____ The most expensive land.

_____ A good community feeling.

_____ Children playing outside in the street.

_____ New neighbours to the area.

_____ A golf course nearby.

_____ Old buildings being demolished.

_____ Find cars speeding.

_____ Live in a cul-de-sac.

_____ Be near a farm.

_____ Buy a new house on a brownfield site.

_____ Find boarded-up houses.

_____ Find well-planned and expensive housing.

_____ Hear people complain about newcomers to the area.

_____ Find people who commute to work.

_____ Cheap housing in need of repair.

_____ Hear people complain about being split up from family and friends.

_____ People behind with the rent.

Remember: Be careful when you are working with different 'points of view'. Your thoughts may be based on labels and unfairness, and not on real knowledge!

What are the different land use patterns in towns?

3 Using your local newspaper, find adverts for property and houses for sale in each of the following areas:

♦ central business district

♦ inner city (town)

♦ inner suburbs

♦ outer suburbs.

Cut out the adverts, then label and stick each one in your book or file.

4 Choose one advert only and in your book or file:

♦ stick the picture in the middle of your page

♦ use all that you have learned from this exercise to label the picture

♦ add labels of your own.

Why are there different land use patterns in towns?

Complete Activity 2 on page 70 in the pupil book.

Use the following mark scheme to assess the quality of your answers.
You should award yourself a point for every comment that you included
in your answer that is in the mark scheme.

As you assess your work, add points that you have missed in another colour
to an appropriate place in your work.

Activity	House	Reason 1	Reason 2	Reason 3	Reason 4	Reason 5
2a First-time home buyer.	1	Price: £100,000	Size: 2 bedrooms.	Location: Close to CBD for jobs and entertainment.	State: Young people could take on modernisation.	Character: Lots of other young people around.
2b Family with two children aged under 6 years.	3	Price: £300,000	Size: 3 bedrooms.	Location: Close to primary school.	Character: Has a garden for children to play in.	Character: Cul-de-sac offers a quiet location with little traffic.
2c Family whose children have left home.	4	Price: £650,000	Character: House has a large garden for relaxing or gardening.	Character: Large conservatory for relaxing.	Access: To the golf course and local shopping centre.	Location: In the outer suburbs where it is quiet.
2d Retired.	1, 3 or 4					
2e Your own choice.						

Why does land use in towns change?

As time passes by, the functions and land uses of different parts of a town will change. These affect different groups of people in different ways.

 Read what people say about the issues, advantages and solutions to inner city change below.

 Write each statement's letter in the Venn diagram below in the place that makes sense to you.

A Money from government to improve housing.	**J** Close to schools, hospitals, libraries, banks and offices.
B Urban Development Corporations buying up old land and restoring derelict buildings.	**K** Risk of unemployment.
C Close to work and many jobs in the city centre.	**L** Money to develop old industrial areas into new workshops, factories, shops and offices.
D Lots of smaller, cheaper, flats and houses.	**M** Lots of things to do for all age groups.
E Higher death rates and more illness.	**N** Close to shops, parks, cinemas and entertainment.
F Families with poorly-paid jobs.	**O** Money to local community groups to help them solve problems including crime, drugs and vandalism.
G New industrial and housing areas like London Docklands.	
H More elderly people, single-parent families and children in care.	**P** Money is now spent on houses and offices, not on hospitals or centres for old people.
I Friendly neighbours and a good community spirit.	**Q** The environment is becoming cleaner.

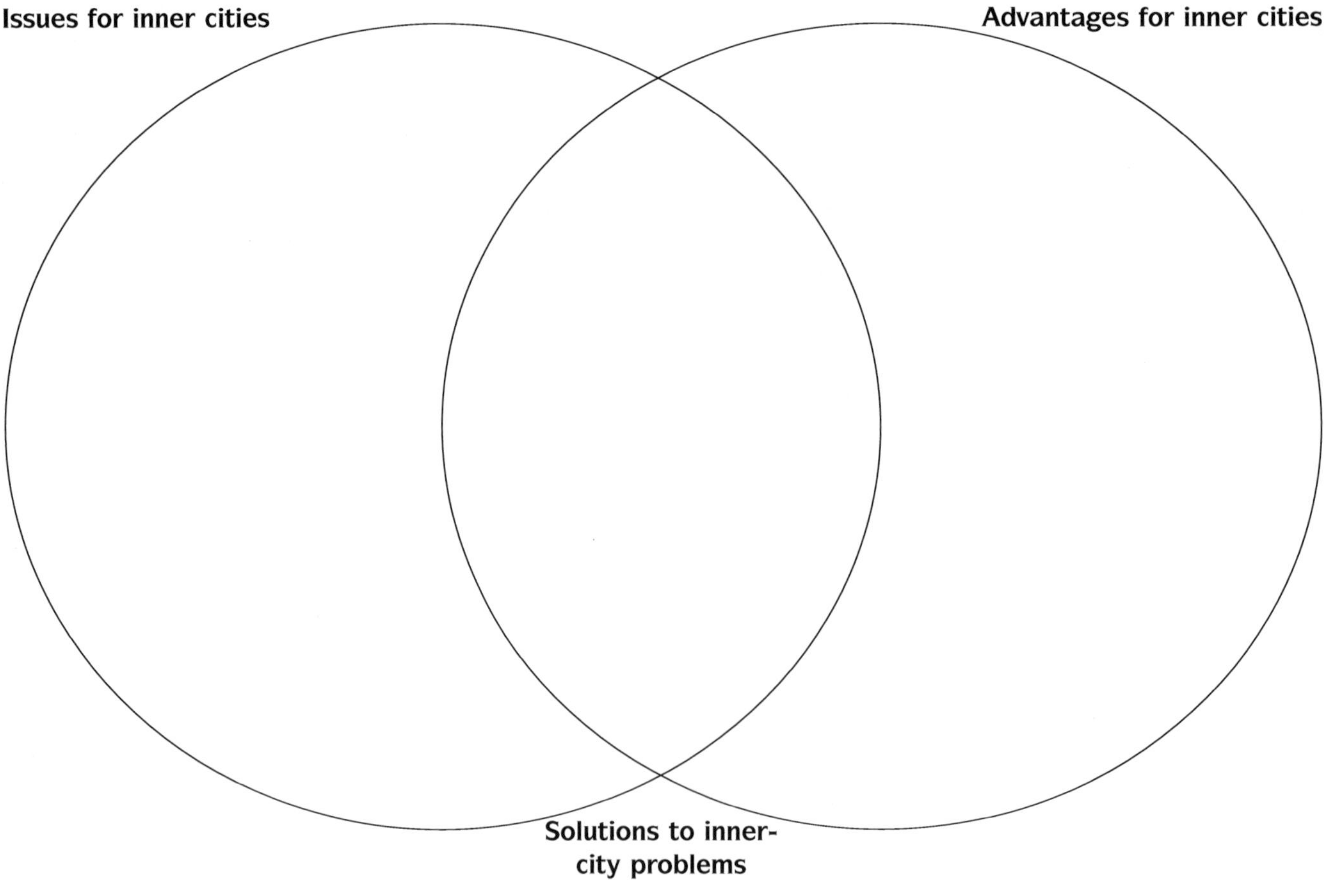

Issues for inner cities   **Advantages for inner cities**

**Solutions to inner-
city problems**

 Write a report on the inner cities for a children's TV programme. This could be presented as a storyboard with images.

Why does land use in towns change?

This activity sheet will help you prepare your thoughts before you complete question 3 on Activity Sheet 4.12 – the report on the inner cities for a children's TV programme. By thinking about how to approach a task before you start it, you are less likely to miss things out and more likely to succeed.

1 Sum up what a high-quality children's TV programme would look and sound like:

_____

_____

_____

2 Write a list of all of the problems being experienced in inner cities.

_____

_____

_____

3 Using the table below, now classify the problems and think about possible solutions.

Problems	Solutions
Economic issues	
Social issues	
Environmental issues	

4 Think of all of the different things that should go into your report. Put a number by each element to show the order you will include them in your report.

You are now ready to make a start on question 3 on Activity Sheet 4.12. Good luck!

Where do we shop?

There are many different types of shopping centre. The larger the centre, the greater the choice of shops and goods there are to buy.

 Look carefully at the photos of different types of shops on page 74 in the pupil book.

 In which photo are you most likely to do the following things? Write each statement's letter in the appropriate place in the Venn diagram below. Place those things that apply to both shops in the overlapping sector.

A Shop two or three times a week.	**N** Find bargains in the January sales.
B Find parking difficult.	**O** Be open late at night.
C Travel here by foot.	**P** Travel here by bus or car.
D Do most of your grocery shopping, once a week.	**Q** Get fed up with the crowds of people.
E Stop for lunch at Macdonald's.	**R** Buy locally-grown vegetables.
F Buy a daily newspaper.	**S** Pay for goods with cash.
G Get caught in a traffic jam.	**T** Have pedestrianised areas.
H Buy new clothes.	**U** Pay more for a pint of milk.
I Have more choice of goods and services.	**V** Use a credit card or storecard.
J Have lower prices.	**W** Buy your weekly Lottery ticket.
K Buy goods less often.	**X** Catch shoplifters on closed-circuit TV.
L Buy exotic fruits from overseas countries.	**Y** Buy a present for someone.
M Find more competition between shops.	**Z** Be near to a main road.

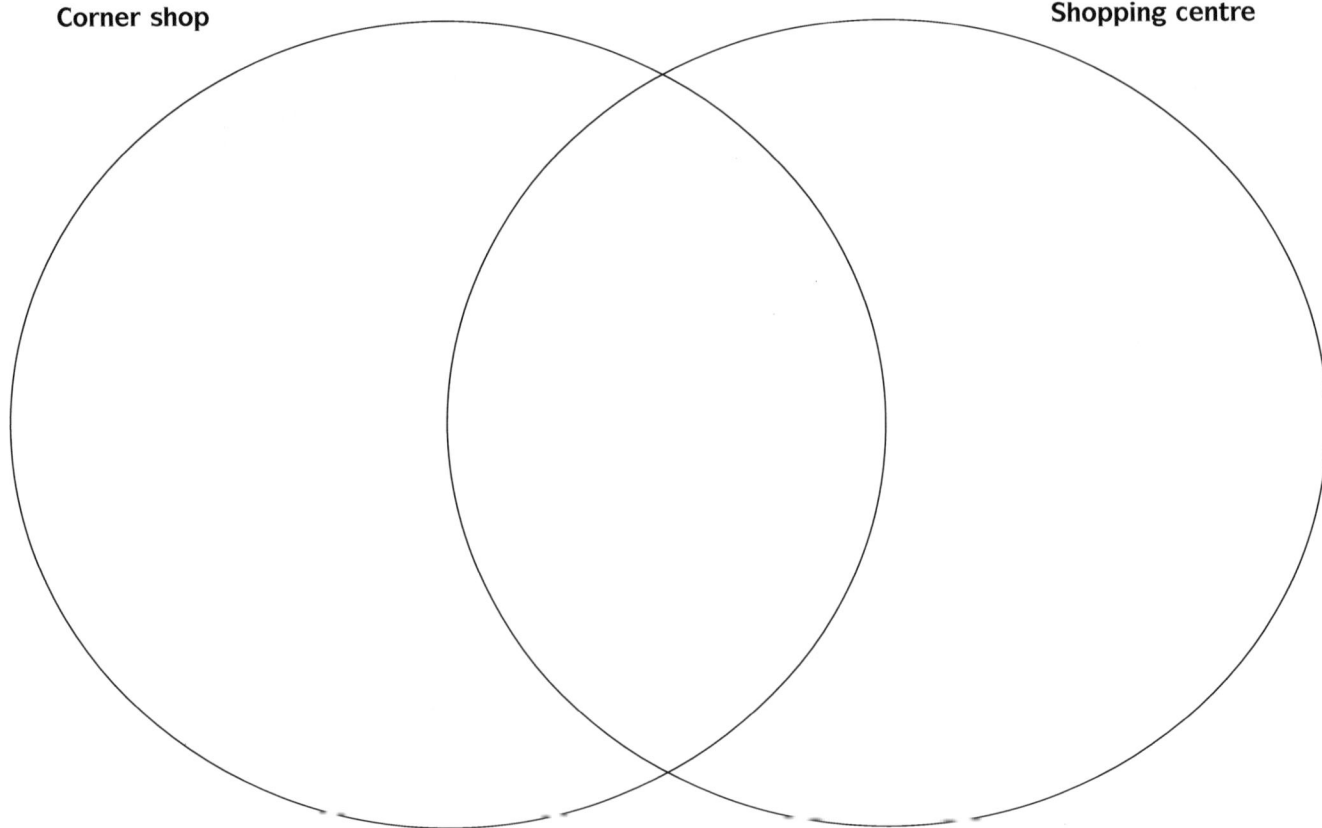

Corner shop

Shopping centre

 Imagine you are a shopkeeper in a corner shop. Write a paragraph to describe 'My customers'.

How has shopping changed?

Shopping habits are changing. The town centre has always been the main shopping area in a town but it is now often congested and expensive. As more people shop by car, modern out-of-town centres are becoming increasingly popular.

 1 Study the following seven labels and write each one in the correct place on the timeline below.

♦ Street markets selling fruit, vegetables, clothing and other things in the open air.

♦ New pedestrianised shopping centres in the CBD with department stores and chain stores. You can't park outside them!

♦ Internet shopping selling virtual goods!

♦ Corner shops, shopping parades and town centres. You might find kerbside parking.

♦ District shopping centres with a variety of shops and a wide choice of goods serving a large area in the suburbs with its own car park.

♦ Out-of-town shopping centres are often huge with chain stores, free car parking, cafés, restaurants and a wide range of leisure amenities.

♦ Shopping streets – main roads lined with shops, leading towards the town centre with car parking for short periods.

Timeline

```
2010 _____
     _____
     _____
     _____
2000 _____
     _____
     _____
     _____
1999 _____
     _____
     _____
     _____
1980 _____
     _____
     _____
     _____
1970 _____
     _____
     _____
     _____
1960 _____
     _____
     _____
     _____
1950 _____
```

 2 How do you think the internet will change shopping in the future?

How does internet shopping work?

The internet has made shopping easier for many people. Its growth may affect the trade of traditional shopping outlets but it can also help reduce congestion and pollution in towns.

 1 Complete the diagram below that shows how internet shopping works by writing the letters of each of the following statements in the correct place.

A The order is sent to the company's distribution warehouse in minutes.

B Connect to a company's website and choose the goods or services that you want.

C The order is received by the company which then confirms details and costs.

D It is finally delivered to your door.

E The order is sent instantly through the internet to the company.

F The order is processed and packed for posting.

G Place your order and give your credit card number and address details for payment.

H The order is transported by plane, van or lorry.

How internet shopping works

 2 'From mouse to house!' Imagine that you are setting up a virtual shop – an internet shop. What will you call your business? What are you going to sell? Make up a name for your company and design a home page for your website.

How does internet shopping affect us?

The internet has made shopping easier for many people. Its growth may affect the trade of traditional shopping outlets but it can also help reduce congestion and pollution in towns.

 In the space below, draw two graphs to show the value (£ million) of internet shopping in each sector for 1999 and 2005. Decide on a scale for your axes.

 Explain how the value of internet shopping is different from one retail sector to another.

Value of internet shopping (£ million)		
Retail sector	**1999**	**2005**
All retail shopping	600	12,500
Grocery	165	4,700
Clothing and footwear	5	1,850
Computer software	120	1,500
Electrical	20	1,000
Music and video	85	780
Books	110	475
Health and beauty	1	350
Other	80	1,325

Explain what happened to the value of internet shopping between 1999 and 2005.

Can you convince Mum to shop online?

Your Mum is not convinced about internet shopping. Compose an argument that you think might just convince your Mum that she could benefit from shopping online.

Below is a table to show what level of detail you need to be successful.

	Number of points made for internet shopping	Number of potential concerns tackled
An excellent answer	6	4
A reasonable answer	4	2
A disappointing answer	3	1

Do not forget that you are trying to convince your Mum. Do not include disadvantages.

_____

_____

_____

_____

_____

_____

_____

_____

_____

_____

_____

_____

_____

_____

_____

_____

_____

_____

_____

_____

_____

_____

_____

Traffic in urban areas – why is it a problem?

Congestion and pollution are major problems in urban areas. The main causes of these problems are too many cars, rush-hour traffic and unsuitable roads.

 1 Study events **A–G** listed below. Each event is linked to a time of day on the traffic flow into London graph on a typical weekday.

Traffic flow into London

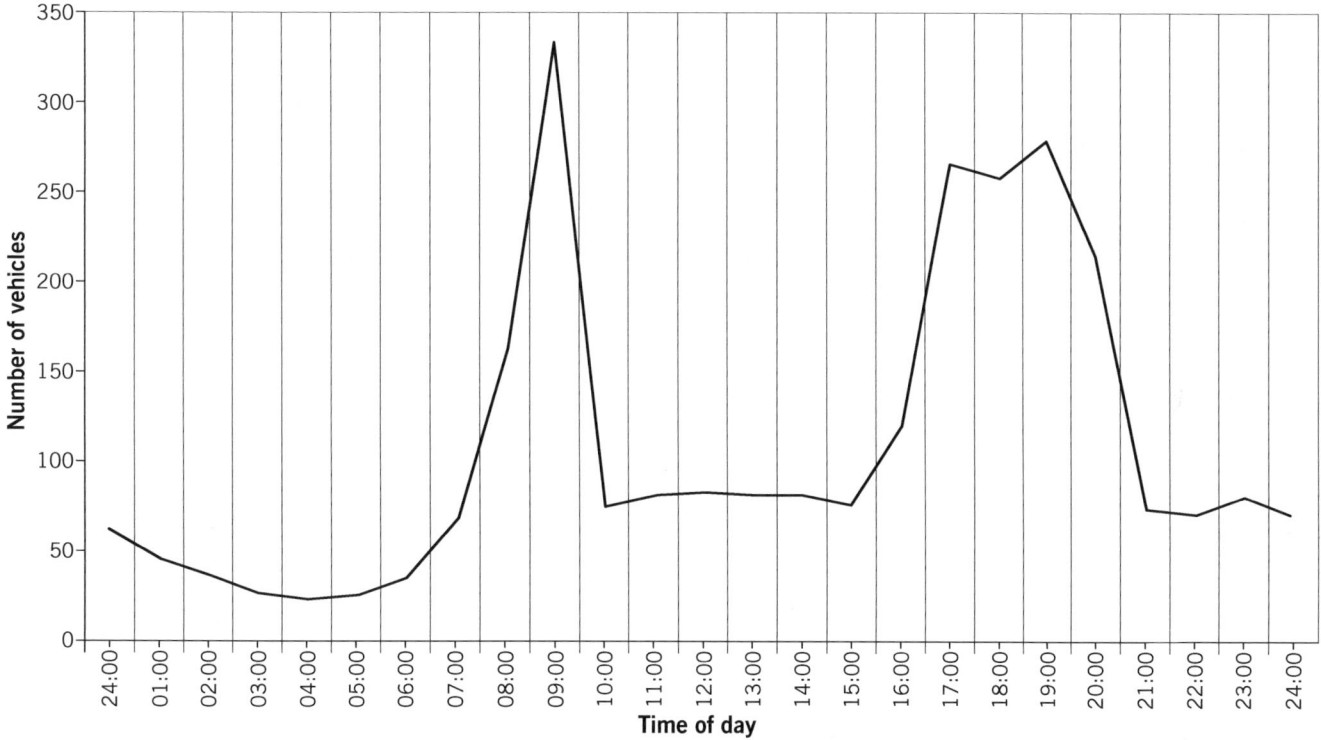

A Grant returns home by bicycle avoiding the heavy evening traffic queues by using the cycle routes.

B Francesca commutes to work, leaving home at dawn for her long journey into the city centre avoiding the congestion charge.

C Carlos gets up late for work and leaves home dreading the traffic congestion and gridlock ahead.

D Yasmin takes her daughter to primary school in her 4x4 vehicle through the infamous 'school run' traffic.

E Despite the long traffic jams, Aki's bus, using the bus lanes, arrives on time in the city centre.

F Maria decides to go shopping for the day after the morning rush hour is over.

G Gennaro takes advantage of his flexitime job and leaves work for home avoiding the evening rush hour.

H _____
_____
_____

 2 Match each event in the list above, to the correct time of day on the traffic flow into London graph.

 3 Compare the shape of the graph and the number of vehicles at the morning and evening rush hours. Why are they different?

 4 Add one more event in the list and graph above.

Traffic in urban areas – gridlock on the roads

1 Read the extract below through for pleasure and to get a general impression. Then read it slowly and carefully again.

2 Answer the following questions as briefly and as clearly as you can:
- Who is speaking in the extract?
- Is the author speaking to anyone? If so, to whom?
- What, in a sentence, is the extract about?
- What is the mood of the extract – happy, sad, frightening, sinister, exciting?

3 Make a list of the images or word-pictures in the extract.

4 In your own words, describe at least two of these images as fully as you can. You may illustrate your work if you wish.

5 Make a list of the words you do not understand. Look up their meanings. Try them in the extract. Do they help?

6 Select a line or phrase you do not fully understand, or a sentence that may mean more than it seems at first reading. Write it out – try one or two explanations – look for clues in the extract. Why, if you think it is a significant sentence, were your suspicions aroused?

7 Think about the following questions:
- Is there a message in the extract? If so, what do you think it is?
- Does the extract remind you of anything you have seen or experienced?
- Is the extract trying to make you think?
- Is the extract making a point? If so, what?
- Does the point go beyond the extract itself?
- What, if anything, did you like about the extract? Explain why and quote from the extract in your explanation.

The problem was one of transport.

The Brainians could see the long, thin arteries along which the humans travelled. They noted that after sunrise the humans all travelled one way and at sunset they all travelled the other. They could see that progress was slow and congested along these arteries, that there were endless blockages, queues, bottlenecks and delays causing untold frustration and inefficiency. All this they could see quite clearly.

What was not clear to them was why.

They knew that humanity was stupid, they only had to look at the week's top ten grossing movies to work that out, but this was beyond reason. If, as was obvious, space was so restricted, why was it that each single member of this strange lifeform insisted on occupying perhaps 50 times its own ground surface area for the entire time it was in motion – or not in motion, as was normally the case?

Extract from *Gridlock* by Ben Elton (Time Warner Book Group UK, 1991)

Traffic in urban areas – the bad news

Congestion and pollution are major problems in urban areas.
The main causes of these problems are too many cars, rush-hour traffic and unsuitable roads.

Below is a list of words to do with traffic.

1	Traffic jams.	10	Too many cars.	19	Traffic lights.
2	Park and Ride schemes.	11	'Sleeping' policemen.	20	Taxis.
3	Bus passes.	12	Accidents.	21	One-way systems.
4	Road rage.	13	By-pass.	22	School runs.
5	Wheel clamps.	14	Pedestrianised streets.	23	Unsuitable, narrow roads.
6	Cycle tracks.	15	Ring road.	24	Rush-hour traffic.
7	Dirty fuel.	16	Shopping trips.	25	Speed cameras.
8	Harmful exhaust fumes.	17	Lack of parking spaces.	26	Double yellow lines.
9	Noise.	18	Multi-storey car parks.	27	Bus lanes.

 a Working with a partner, study the sets of numbers below, which match to words in the list above.

b Cross out the 'odd one out' in each set.

c Add a fourth number to match the other two.

d Explain what links the three 'in' numbers.

Set A	1	22	9	
What's the link?				
Set B	2	16	15	
What's the link?				
Set C	27	6	13	
What's the link?				
Set D	24	12	19	
What's the link?				
Set E	15	27	5	
What's the link?				
Set F				
What's the link?				
Set G				
What's the link?				

 Add two more sets to the table and ask a partner to find the 'odd one out' and explain what links the other three numbers.

Why traffic in urban areas has become a problem

Sort the following statements to explain how an increase in traffic can cause many other problems. Agree a correct order for the statements as a class

and complete a copy of the negative multiplier diagram below. The first box has been completed for you.

There are now eight times more cars than 50 years ago	Traffic jams are blocking roads and stopping all movement	As a result of traffic jams, the police, fire and ambulance services say lives are put at risk
The speed with which people and goods can move around the country is slowed down	Businesses then lose money and are put off moving to busy areas	Congestion and growing frustration causes an increase in road traffic accidents
People and buildings are affected by the noise	By 2025, the number of cars may be double and lorries three times what they are now	Harmful exhaust fumes affect people's health

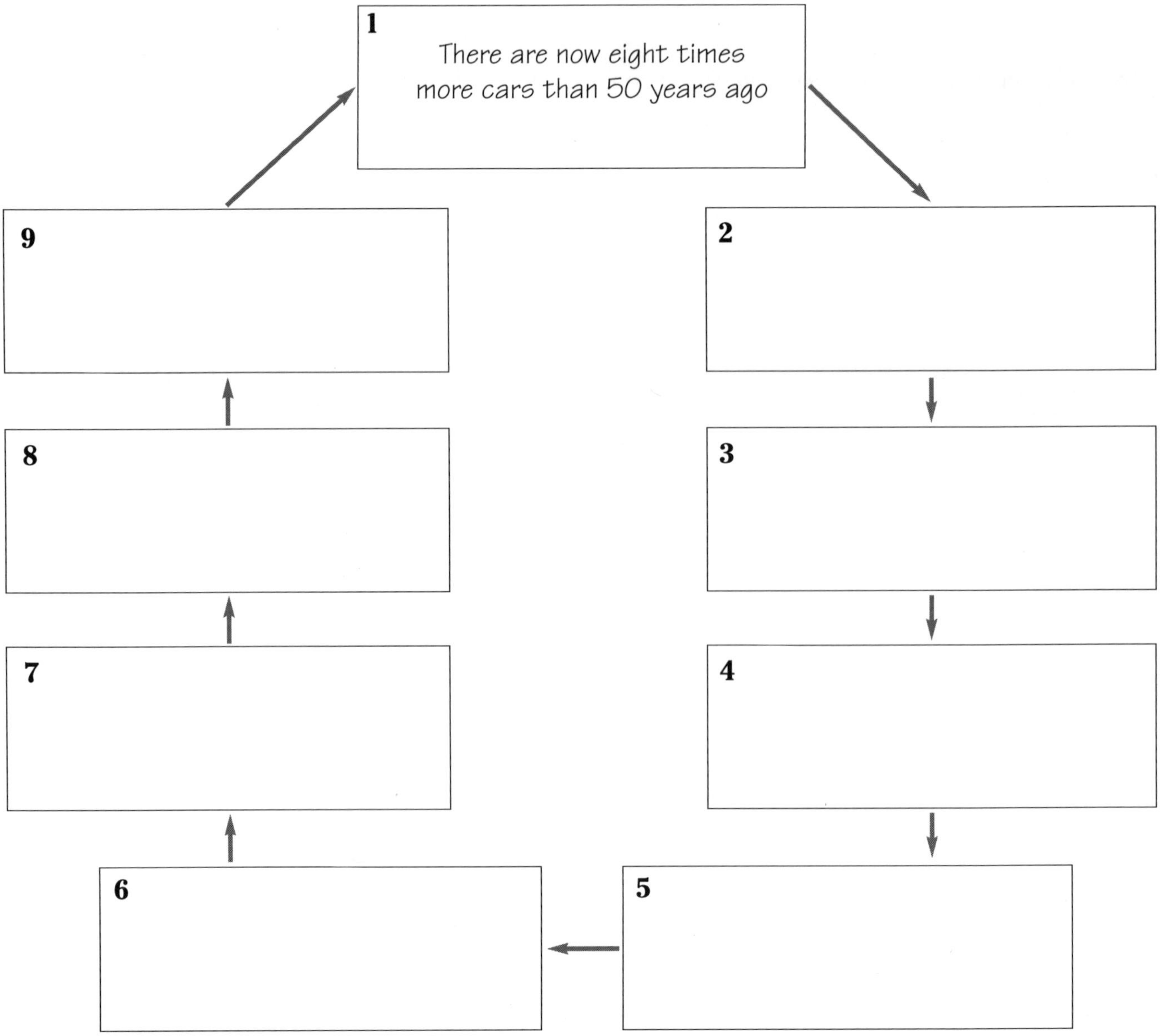

1 There are now eight times more cars than 50 years ago

9

2

8

3

7

4

6

5

Traffic in urban areas – is there a solution?

Solving the problem of urban traffic is difficult. Better public transport may be the best way to improve people's movements without further damaging the environment. People have different views on how to ease the growing problem of traffic congestion.

 Working with a partner, complete the Venn diagram below by sorting statements 1–30 into the problems and solutions of traffic congestion. Write each statement's number in the appropriate place. Statements that relate to the causes of traffic congestion can be placed in the overlapping sector.

1   Better traffic management.
2   Parking permits.
3   Improve public transport.
4   Develop rail routes.
5   More by-passes.
6   Air pollution.
7   Cheaper fares.
8   Park and Ride schemes.
9   Fewer car parks
10 Make car parking expensive.
11 Multi-storey car parks.

12 Parking meters.
13 Speed limits of 10 mph.
14 Commuters.
15 Cycle routes.
16 Traffic jams and grid-locked roads.
17 More off-street parking.
18 More motorways.
19 Driver stress.
20 Reduce public transport fares.
21 Congestion charging and road tolling.
22 Build more roads.

23 Raise the price of petrol.
24 Frequent bus services and bus lanes.
25 One-way systems to help traffic to move.
26 Pedestrianised shopping areas.
27 Breathing problems caused by car fumes.
28 Traffic calming with speed bumps.
29 Loss of land for road widening.
30 Flexitime for workers.

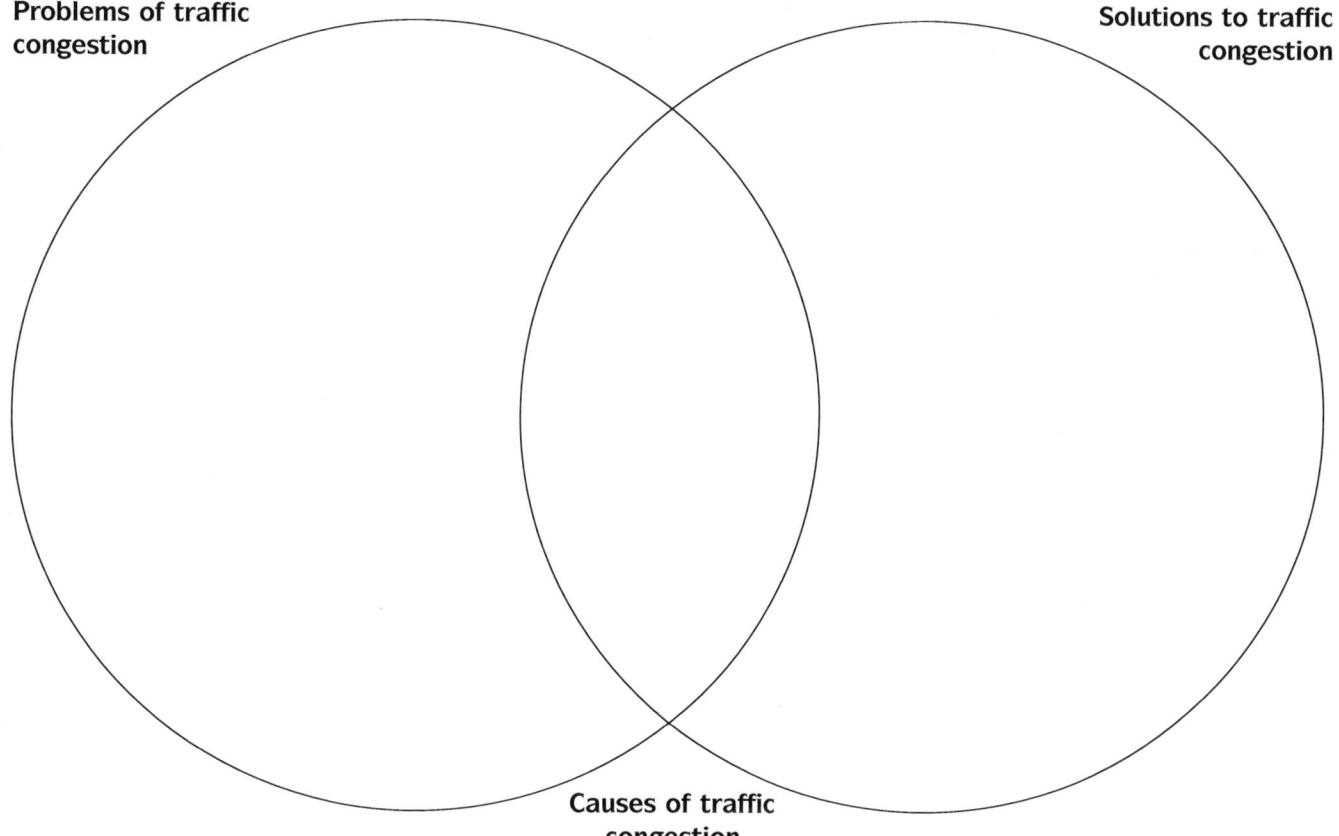

Problems of traffic congestion

Solutions to traffic congestion

Causes of traffic congestion

 Do you think that private cars should be:
 ◆ kept out of all towns
 ◆ kept out of some areas
 ◆ allowed to go wherever they wish?
Explain your answer.

 Road congestion and car parking are two of the biggest problems in urban areas. One idea to help solve this problem is to build more car parks. Is this a good idea? Explain your answer.

Traffic in urban areas – solutions?

Write or cut out and arrange the signs and statements below on to a
large piece of paper so that there is plenty of space between them.

Draw lines between the statements that are linked. Along each line write
what the link is. For example: 'Park and Ride schemes reduce the
number of cars on the road because people park outside of the city
centre and travel by bus.'

Bus stop

Reduces traffic fumes

M

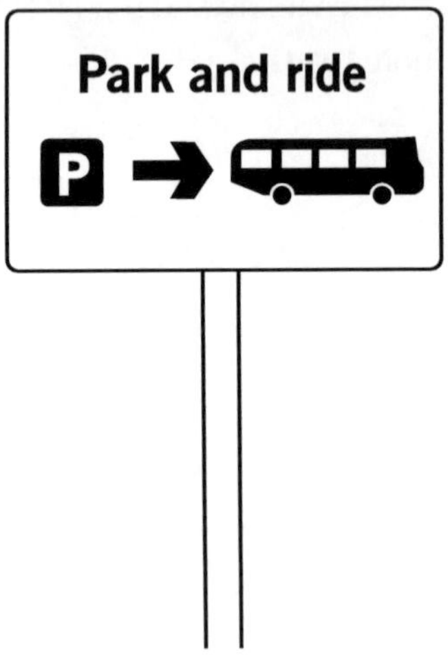

Park and ride

Speeds up journey times
for passengers

Reduces the number of
cars on the road

Slows traffic down,
increasing safety

Transport
for London

**Congestion
charging**

C

**Central
ZONE**

Mon - Fri
7 am - 6.30 pm

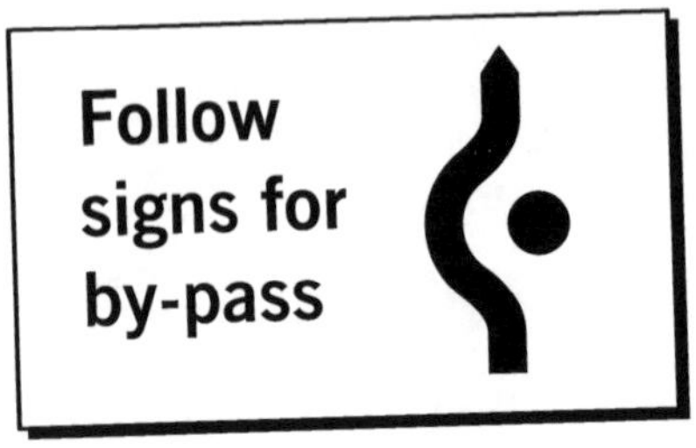

**Follow
signs for
by-pass**

Is a quick, cheap and
easy solution

Where should the by-pass go?

When a place becomes too crowded with vehicles, a road can be built around it to take away some of the traffic. A road that is built to avoid a congested area is called a by-pass.

 Working with a partner, carefully read through the statements below.

 Decide whether each statement is a **Fact** or an **Opinion** and tick the appropiate box.

	Fact	Opinion
A by-pass will mean more traffic on country roads.		
There is a rush hour every day as people drive to and from their work.		
Lots of wildlife will be driven away.		
It will not solve congestion when it is finished because traffic will simply increase.		
A by-pass means that through traffic will not have to go into town.		
When cars are stuck in queues, travelling slowly, they give off exhaust fumes.		
Heavy traffic going through towns causes vibration, which damages the foundations of buildings.		
It will cause traffic chaos while work is being done.		
It will mean less peace in the countryside.		
If traffic is moving too slowly, it causes firms to lose money.		
If ambulances are delayed, it can be a danger to the public.		
By-passes are blocked at rush hours every working day.		
The rush hour can cause accidents leading to injury and loss of life.		
Trees will have to be cut down.		
Nice green views will be ruined.		
The millions of pounds it will cost would be better spent on other things.		
Road work or a minor accident can cause tailbacks of many miles.		
There will be less land for farming.		
Many trees will be cut down.		
The area will look better.		
Building a new road will only increase the amount of traffic.		
More countryside will be covered in concrete.		
Vehicles slowing down, stopping and starting use extra fuel and cause more air pollution.		
A local beauty spot and picnic area will be destroyed.		

 'Traffic increases to fill the space available.'
What do you think this means?

Where should the Haydon Bridge by-pass go?

Now you have completed Activity 1 on page 84 in the pupil book to decide where the Haydon Bridge by-pass should go, it is time to inform the local council of your decision.

Produce a presentation to the council at Haydon Bridge which:

◆ clearly states which route you think the by-pass should take

◆ explains, using a number of reasons, why you think this route would be best

◆ refers to people who would benefit from the chosen route

◆ outlines at least one reason why you think the other routes were not appropriate.

Before you start your presentation, brainstorm all of the things that make a good presentation. These will become your success criteria. Write these in a copy of the table below.

You will assess one of the other presentations and provide feedback to that group.

Success criteria	Did you see or hear it in the presentation?	Evaluation comments, e.g. 'We liked…', 'We thought it would have been good if you…'
1		
2		
3		
4		
5		

The settlement enquiry

Before you finish your enquiry, use the reminders below to make sure you have covered all of the correct points.

Success criteria	A helpful resource	Self evaluation	Teacher evaluation
1 Make sure your work is laid out like an official letter.			
2 Outline the problems that used to exist.	Analyse Figure **A** on page 87 in the pupil book.		
3 Describe the problems identified by your first environmental quality survey.	Activity 3b on page 86 in the pupil book.		
4 Make some recommendations about which of these problems you think is a priority to tackle first.	Look at Figures **A** and **B** on page 87 in the pupil book. What if you could only make one change?		
5 Describe what could be done to improve the area.	Analyse Figure **B** on page 87 in the pupil book.		
6 Explain how you think the quality of the environment would change by using your results from the second survey.	Compare the results of your first environmental quality survey with the second you did. In which section of the survey did the score improve?		
7 Comment on your opinion.	Look carefully at both diagrams. Which do you prefer and why?		
8 List the other groups of people who you think would agree with you.	Use the people at the bottom of page 87 in the pupil book.		
9 Explain how these people would benefit.	Look carefully at Figure **B** on page 87 in the pupil book. How would life be easier for these people?		
10 Include a conclusion.			
11 Check your spelling and punctuation.			

Think about your learning!

Before you submit your final enquiry, spend some time thinking about the learning that you have carried out.

1 Look carefully at this list of skills. Geographers are skilled people! **Tick** the skills you are developing during your time working on this enquiry.

2 Describe **one** thing that enabled you to be successful in this task:

_____

_____

_____

_____

3 Describe **one** problem you had, or thought you had, that stopped you from achieving your potential:

_____

_____

_____

_____

_____

Teamwork	☐
Reading	☐
Listening	☐
Discussion	☐
Problem solving	☐
Decision making	☐
Map interpretation	☐
Graphing	☐
Data analysis	☐
Questioning	☐
Debating	☐
Time management	☐
Presenting	☐
Empathy	☐
Annotation	☐
Evaluation	☐
Research	☐
Using ICT	☐
Comparing	☐

4 In these boxes write **two** actions that you will carry out to help you be more successful and reach your target in the future.

5 The Indian Ocean tsunami — *Unit Overview*

Approximate teaching time, 10 hours

KEY IDEAS:

◆ the causes of the earthquake and tsunami
◆ the effects of the tsunami

◆ how the world responded to the disaster
◆ how the tsunami danger may be reduced.

Pos	Key questions	Pupil book	Suggested activities/methods
6b ii, 6b iii, 6c ii	The world's worst natural disaster?	88, 89	Pupils could be asked for their own recollection of the disaster, or the emergency relief that followed. If this is too long in the past, discuss with pupils what natural disasters from the past they are able to recall.
6b ii, 6b iii, 6c ii	What caused the Asian tsunami of December, 2004?	90, 91	Discussion of the causes of the tsunami. Link to prior learning on earthquakes.
6b iii, 6c ii	How did the tsunami affect different countries?	92, 93	Analysis of the effects of the tsunami on different countries, relating this to location and distance from the initial earthquake.
6b ii, 6c ii	What were the effects of the tsunami?	94, 95	Analysis of the main short and long-term effects of the tsunami.
6b iii, 6c ii	How did the world help?	96, 97	Discussion of the impacts of emergency relief, short-term aid and long-term aid.
6b iii, 6c ii	How can the tsunami danger be reduced?	98, 99	Analysis of the effectiveness of prediction and preparation as means of reducing the impact of tsunamis.
6b iii, 6c ii	Tsunami enquiry – what help can be given to people affected by the tsunami?	100, 101	Pupils prioritise spending on various projects within a finite budget.

PoS	Skills
1	Geographical enquiry and skills
1e	Appreciate the importance of values and attitudes
2d	Select and use secondary sources of evidence
2g	Decision-making skills

Vocabulary and technical terms

(see Glossary in pupil book)

Earthquake
Emergency relief/aid
Hazard
Long-term

Plates
Tsunami
Short-term

Assessment for Learning

Pages 90–97: Activity Sheets 5.9a and b

Pupils should work in pairs. They should pick and place statements alternately. As each statement is placed, pupils should orally justify why they have chosen to locate the statement in that particular column.

Differentiation

Reduce the activity by asking pupils to find three statements to go in each column of the table.

Extension

Ask pupils to begin completing the table from memory. They can then use the statements to check the accuracy of their knowledge and add any statements they have missed. The causes could be numbered so that they are listed in the correct order. The effects could be further classified into short-term and long-term effects and social, economic and environmental effects. The examples of management could be further classified into emergency relief, short-term aid, long-term aid and disaster reduction.

Pages 90–97: Activity Sheet 5.9c

Choose a pupil to justify the location of one of the statements. Write their answer on the board. Ask other pupils to improve the answer by adding/removing words. Alternatively, ask other pupils to counter argue the first pupil's answer.

Differentiation

Reduce the activity by asking pupils to explain the location of one or two statements.

Extension

Pupils should explain why a particular statement cannot be placed in the other two columns.

Pages 98–99: Activity Sheets 5.12a–c

This activity is best suited to mixed-ability groups of four pupils. There are two sets of domino cards, one about prediction and one about preparation. Groups should be given one set or the other. After they have arranged the dominoes, pupils need to collate information in preparation for a short presentation to the rest of the class.

Assessment for Learning

As pupils place a domino down, they must explain their reasons to the rest of their group. If the group agrees, it can be placed. If not, another domino should be chosen.

Differentiation

Pupils with particular abilities can be matched to particular parts of the presentation. For example, more-able pupils may be better suited to answering the last question which asks them to think of their own recommendations for reducing the effects of the tsunami.

Extension

Groups could be asked to think of other recommendations for reducing the effects of a tsunami.

Pages 100–101: Activity Sheet 5.13

In order to answer Activity 2 on page 100 of the pupil book, pupils need to analyse which of the schemes on page 101 meet the aims of the Disaster Emergency Agency. Activity Sheet 5.13 will enable pupils to complete this task in a simple and clear manner. Once pupils have placed ticks in what they think are the appropriate boxes, they can compare their answers with their peers. If they disagree on whether or not a particular scheme meets a particular aim, they can discuss their viewpoints to clarify their understanding. This may lead to one pupil changing their mind. This process of checking their work deepens understanding of both pupils and will increase their confidence in the quality of their answers before they continue with the remainder of the task.

Pages 100–101: The tsunami enquiry

The tsunami enquiry Checklist (page 154) can be used in two ways.

1   It can be used by pupils to check whether or not they have met the success criteria for the enquiry. As they complete each task, pupils can tick the parts they have completed. If there are any parts not ticked, the pupils can be sure of what they need to include to complete the enquiry. Because the Checklist has elements that the pupils *should* and *could* complete, it will give pupils clear guidance as to how they can improve their enquiry.

2   The Checklist can also be used by an assessor (either a teacher or another pupil if an element of peer marking is to be introduced) to mark pupils' work. Once again, the boxes that remain empty will diagnose where the pupil has failed to meet the criteria. The work could be returned to the pupil once an assessor has looked at the work so that any omissions can be corrected by the pupil. This process of drafting work is an important skill for geographers and will breed good habits for future years.

What are natural disasters?

Disasters may be described as being man-made, like an air crash, or natural, like earthquakes and volcanoes.

Below is a list of words about disasters.

1	Hurricane.	**14**	Crop failure.	**27**	Refugee.
2	Avalanche.	**15**	Tornado.	**28**	Willy-willies.
3	Ice storm.	**16**	Malnutrition.	**29**	Monsoon.
4	Blizzard.	**17**	Drought.	**30**	Cholera.
5	Snow.	**18**	Mosquito.	**31**	Heat wave.
6	Heavy rain.	**19**	Earthquake.	**32**	Malaria.
7	High tides.	**20**	Landslide.	**33**	Terrorism.
8	Flood.	**21**	Air crash.	**34**	Lava flow.
9	Snow melt.	**22**	Tsunami.	**35**	Hostage.
10	Deforestation.	**23**	Homelessness.	**36**	Volcanic eruption.
11	Cyclone.	**24**	Smog.	**37**	Forest fire.
12	Typhoon.	**25**	Poverty.	**38**	Epidemic.
13	Famine.	**26**	War.	**39**	AIDS.

 a Working with a partner, study the sets of numbers below, which match to words in the list above.

b Cross out the 'odd one out' in each set.

c Add a fourth number to match the other two.

d Explain what links the three 'in' numbers.

Set A	4	29	6	
What's the link?				
Set B	1	28	24	
What's the link?				
Set C	7	11	17	
What's the link?				
Set D	19	36	21	
What's the link?				
Set E	31	8	37	
What's the link?				
Set F	2	29	9	
What's the link?				
Set G				
What's the link?				

 Add one more set to the table and ask a partner to find the 'odd one out' and explain what links the other three numbers.

The world's worst natural disaster?

You are the editor for a national newspaper. News has just come in of a major natural disaster – the tsunami earthquake. You have to design and write the front page to report the event. You can either use the page layout below or design your own. A word processor or DTP program will make your page look more professional.

Front-page layout design

Make up your own newspaper name.

To attract people to your story.

To introduce your article on causes of earthquakes and tsunamis.

Simple line drawing to show tsunami or damage done.

Description of how the tsunami affected different countries.

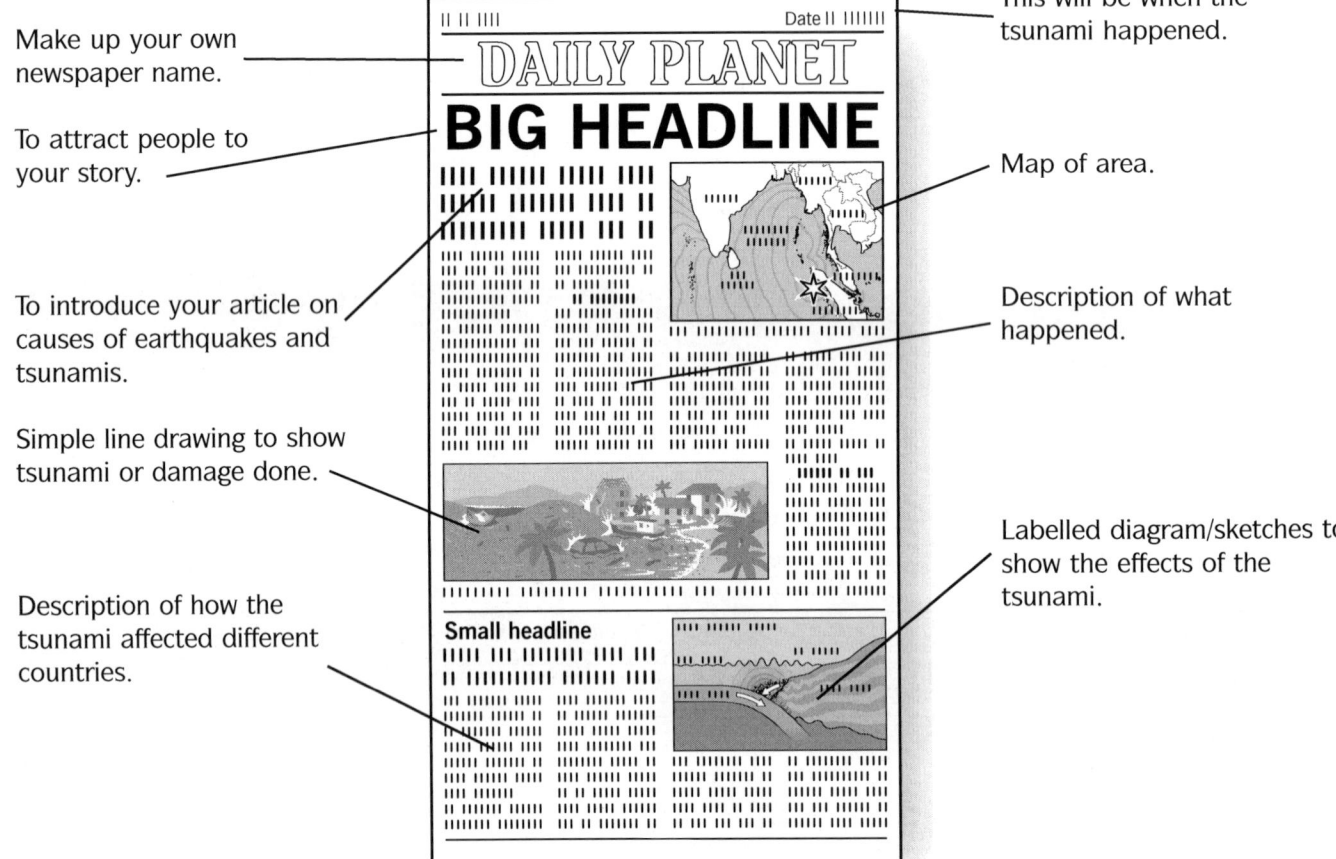

This will be when the tsunami happened.

Map of area.

Description of what happened.

Labelled diagram/sketches to show the effects of the tsunami.

What caused the tsunami?

At 8 am on 26 December 2004, a massive earthquake below the Indian Ocean caused giant waves called tsunamis. These tsunamis caused terrible damage and more than 300,000 people died. The earthquake occurred off the west coast of Northern Sumatra, an island of Indonesia. The tsunami waves hit 12 coastal countries in the area. The floods caused by the tsunamis mixed the water in the sewers with wells and other sources of drinking water. Millions of people did not have clean water to drink. The tsunamis also destroyed hundreds of thousands of family homes and food supplies. One out of every three people affected by this disaster is a child.

Imagine that you are a newspaper reporter assigned to report on the tsunami disaster. On your way to the devastated area you must plan your research and press release.

What was the damage?

When did it happen?

Where did it happen?

How were the people affected?

Who was affected?

Why did it happen?

1. Working with a partner or in a small group, study the photo and questions above.

2. Think of more questions to help you find out what is happening and to help the newspaper's readers to understand the disaster. Add questions around the edge of the photo to those already there. Your questions should begin with: What? Where? Who? When? Why? How?

3. Try to answer as many of the questions as possible. You may need to refer to the pupil book or even do some further research.

The earth's continental plates

The outer layer of the earth is like a jigsaw. It is broken into huge pieces called plates. Each plate moves in its own direction. A massive earthquake off the coast of Sumatra produced the Indian Ocean tsunami. Two plates colliding with each other caused the earthquake.

Cut out the shapes below. Then fit them together to make the plates of the earth's crust.

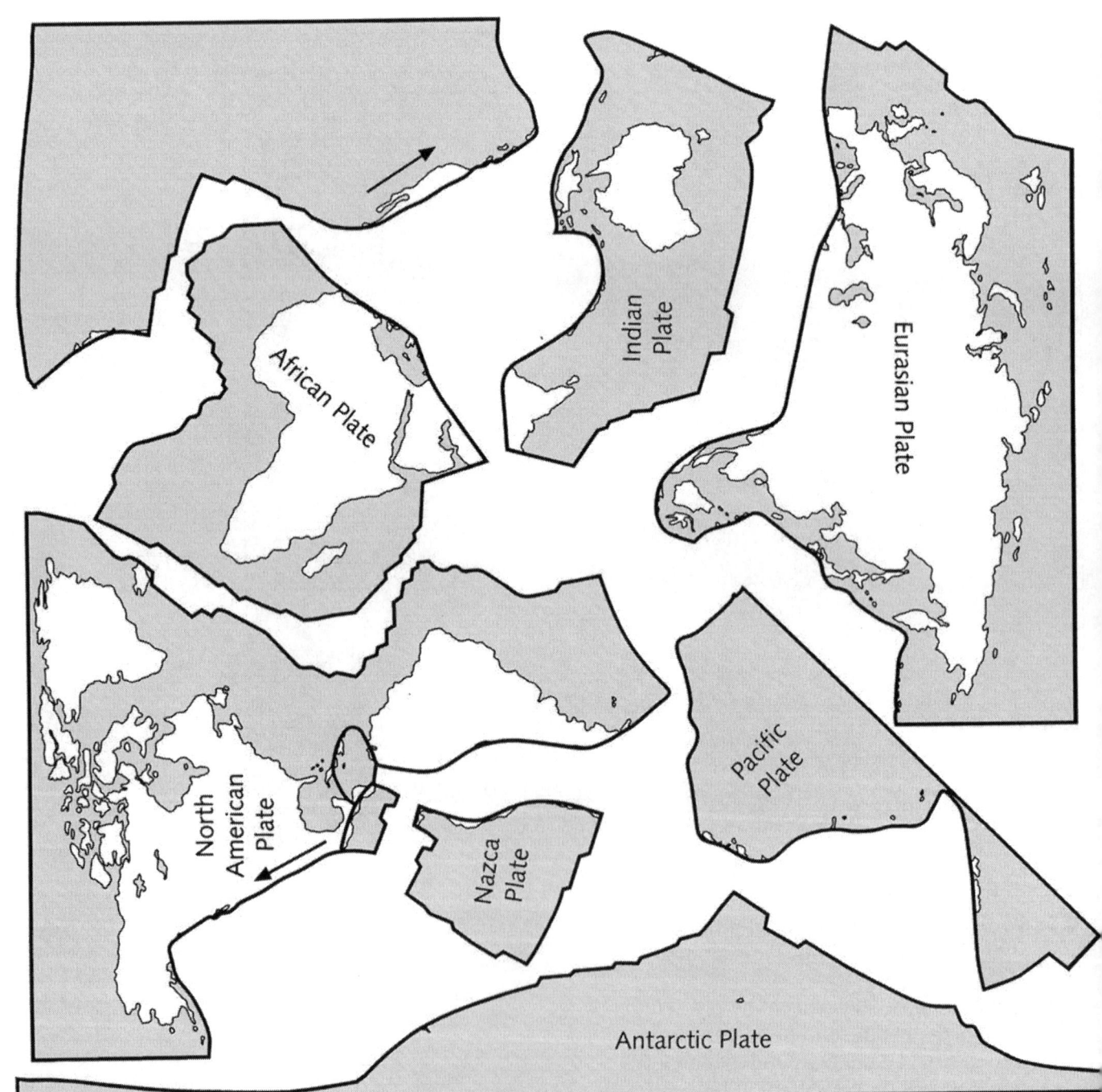

Eye-witness accounts of the tsunami

As a newspaper reporter, you must now interview people affected by the tsunami.

In turn, imagine that you are each of the people mentioned below. Complete each sentence as if you were being interviewed.

Homeowner: I have lost everything I own _____

_____

Mother: I was preparing breakfast when _____

_____

Fisherman: I was mending my nets on the shoreline as the sea suddenly retreated _____

_____

Government representative: I have been sent by the Prime Minister to see for myself _____

_____

Nurse: Hospitals are prepared for disasters but the number of casualties overwhelmed me _____

_____

Rescued victim: I was trapped in the mud and calling for help _____

_____

International Rescue worker: My team arrived on the scene within one day. We saw people digging, using bare hands in search for survivors _____

_____

'Sniffer' dog handler: My dog is specially trained but found it difficult to find buried victims trapped under the debris _____

_____

TV reporter: This must be one of the most terrible sights I have filmed. The devastation is incredible

_____

_____

UN Disaster Relief worker: This is one of the worst natural disasters in living memory. I shall be reporting to the UN that _____

_____

Backpacker: I was lazing on the beach writing a postcard when _____

_____

_____

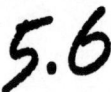

What were the effects of the tsunami?

Your news editor is expecting a press release on the Indian Ocean tsunami today! It is not aimed at the public; so don't copy a newspaper style. You must provide clear and concise information – about one side of A4 – that your editor can use. You can provide extra information at the end in a note to the editor.

The plan of a press release

- Use a word processor.
- Double-space text to allow room for your editor's notes.
- Use only one side of paper.

Date for release
e.g. FOR IMMEDIATE RELEASE

Headline
Keep it simple.

Opening paragraph
Use your research questions from Activity Sheet 5.3:
What has happened? **Where** did it happen? **When** and **why** did it happen?
The reason for the press release.

The introduction
The most interesting fact about the tsunami disaster. This must catch the editor's attention... otherwise your press release may be binned and another reporter's may make the front page!

Main body of press release
- Make the press release easy to read.
- Concentrate on the facts in order of importance; give the number of people involved, spell out first names, quote statistics; do not use bold or underline.
- Use the active voice; don't write: 'my team arrived on the scene within one day said International Rescue worker Alan Tracy'; do write, 'International Rescue worker, Alan Tracy, said that his team arrived on the scene within one day.'
- Use quotes; news is about people – people describing what they have seen, feel and think; every press release should include direct quotation – you can even make up your own.

END
Set this word below the final sentence.
(Use the word 'MORE' if you continue onto another page.)

Contact details and other material
e.g. For further information or to arrange an interview...
perhaps leave a mobile number or e-mail address.

Photos of the disaster are available on request.

How did the world help?

The disaster relief programme was a worldwide effort. It brought both immediate and long-term help in the form of materials, money and expert assistance to the people and countries in most need.

 Arrange all the factors in a pyramid shape, like the one shown below. The final arrangement must be what you decide as a group.

 Working in a group of three or four, cut out each of the 10 statements on Activity Sheet 5.7b.

 Report back to the rest of the class on the choice of your arrangement.

 Now imagine that you are in charge of a relief operation and you have just arrived at the scene of the disaster. You are going to decide as a group in which order the 10 statements must be put into action.

At the *top* of the pyramid, place the statement you think is the most important.

On the *second* line place the two statements that are equal second – not as important as the top one, but more important than the others.

On the *third* line place the three statements that are equal third.

On the *bottom* line, place the four statements that are equal fourth. Just because a factor is on the bottom line, it does not mean that it is not important, just that those above it are more important.

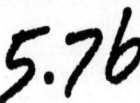

How did the world help?

As soon as you receive the news of the disaster, you send out an urgent appeal for international assistance from doctors, nurses and other medical staff.

It is best to house people as close as possible to their own homes, rather than in make-shift camps.

After the tsunami, individual team members who live in the area should take care of their own family and belongings first.

Through newspapers and TV, you ask people in the UK to collect and send medicines, clothing and equipment.

You ask the local police and the army to guard homes, shops and factories. This will stop people from stealing things while the owners remain missing.

There are limited food supplies and so the young and the old should be given food first.

Food is the top priority, otherwise people will starve.

Even weeks after the disaster you must expect things to be far from back to normal. Most services will not be running properly.

One top priority must be the gathering and disposing of dead bodies, because there is a danger that they will cause infectious diseases.

The disaster will have focused the world's attention on the troubles of the people you have been helping. If a disaster happens here again, it will be easier to raise the resources you need. The disaster will not have such a devastating effect.

Aid and the disaster relief programme

The disaster relief programme was a worldwide effort. It brought both immediate and long-term help in the form of materials, money and expert assistance to the people and countries most in need.

1 a Complete the Venn diagram below by placing each statement's letter in the appropriate place.

b If you think that the example may be emergency relief help, write the letter in the overlapping sector.

A   Clean water.
B   Tents.
C   Food parcels.
D   Canned food.
E   Heat seeking equipment.
F   Clothing.
G   Vaccinations.
H   Heavy-lifting equipment.
I   Baby food.
J   Pneumatic drills.
K   Medical equipment.
L   Teams of doctors and nurses.
M   Blankets.
N   Education and play kits for schools.
O   Counselling for emotionally-distressed children.

P   Computers to help manage relief operation.
Q   Emergency health kits with a shelf life of five years.
R   Money to pay for supplies and rebuilding programmes.
S   Charity organisations launch fundraising schemes.
T   International aid.
U   Toilet and shower porta-cabins, with septic tanks.
V   Skilled people, e.g. engineers, who can give advice.
W   Purification tablets for dirty water.
X   Waterproof heavy-duty plastic.
Y   Rescue workers, 'sniffer dogs' and handlers.
Z   Mosquito bed nets.

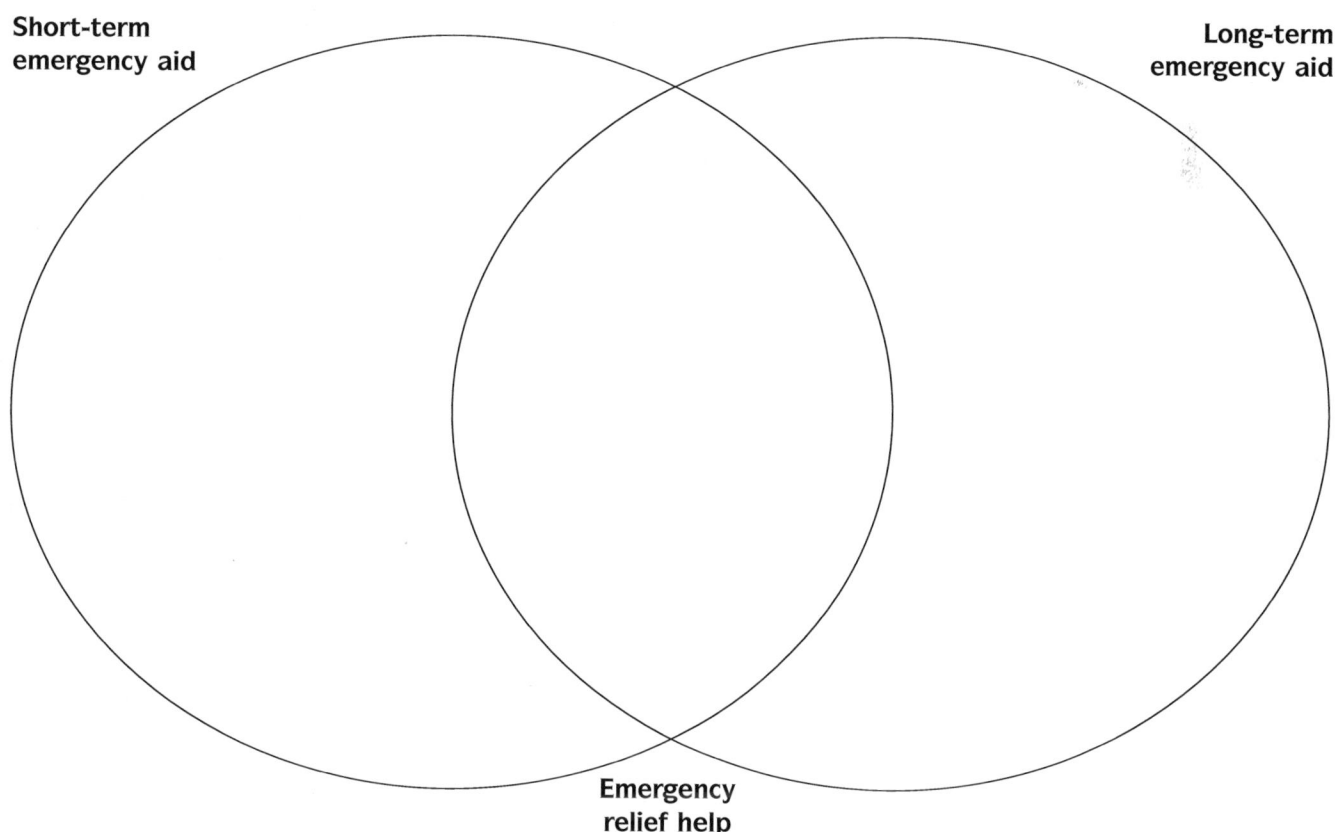

Short-term emergency aid

Long-term emergency aid

Emergency relief help

2 Highlight the main types of aid in the list above as follows:
- Government aid in red.
- Voluntary aid in green.

The causes, effects and management of the tsunami

Copy and complete the table below using the statements on
Activity Sheet 5.9b. Statements relating to:

◆ how the tsunami happened are *causes*

◆ the results of the tsunami are *effects*

◆ what the authorities did to help the people affected are
examples of *management*.

Causes	Effects	Management
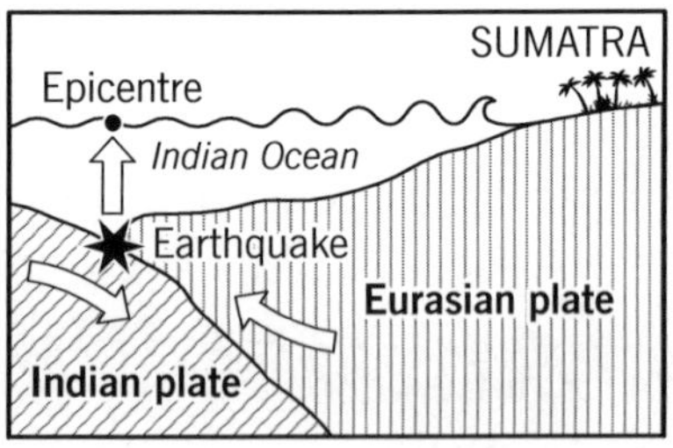 Epicentre, SUMATRA, Indian Ocean, Earthquake, Eurasian plate, Indian plate		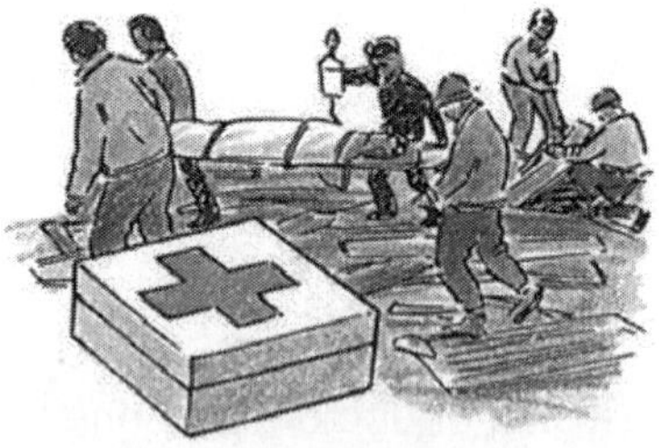

The causes, effects and management of the tsunami

Local authorities are developing disaster plans

Sea above the earthquake is forced upwards

Plate movement causes earthquake

A tsunami early warning system is to be implemented in the Indian Ocean

Tsunami waves travel at up to 800 km/h in deep water

Indian plate moves towards Eurasian plate

1.7 million people made homeless

Many people donated money after TV, radio, newspaper and internet appeals

Over 310,000 people dead or missing

Coastal roads and railways were wrecked

Two million jobs lost

12 countries were seriously affected by the waves

Thailand's tourist industry badly hit as hotels and facilities were damaged

Over 650,000 people seriously injured

Coastal rice fields of Sumatra destroyed by sea water

70% of Indonesian fishing boats destroyed meaning people lost their livelihood

International relief organisations flew blankets, tents, clean water, food and medical supplies into the areas affected

Governments provided trained personnel, helicopters and heavy machinery

Governments promised money for rebuilding schools and hospitals and to restart industries destroyed

The causes, effects and management of the tsunami

Choose three of the statements from Activity Sheet 5.9b and explain why you have located them in a particular place.

Statement 1: _____

I have put this statement in the _____ column because _____

_____

_____

_____

_____

_____

_____

_____

Statement 2: _____

I have put this statement in the _____ column because _____

_____

_____

_____

_____

_____

_____

_____

Statement 3: _____

I have put this statement in the _____ column because _____

_____

_____

_____

_____

_____

_____

_____

How did the world help?

Following major natural disasters, international appeals are set up to help the people affected. These appeals have to be 'hard-hitting' to make sure that they have an immediate impact on their audience. Any such appeals are usually backed-up by posters in national newspapers, TV images, radio messages and web pages.

'Don't take pity – take action!' You are in charge of planning the Asian earthquake appeal. Working with a partner or in a small group, you have a one-minute TV slot to launch an appeal for tsunami disaster victims. Write the script and draw a storyboard to go with it, showing the images you will broadcast.

◆ Think carefully about the screen shots you want to use. You could glue photos into the storyboard or draw pictures, or even write short descriptions of what you would show.

◆ Include a voice over for each frame. Think carefully about the message you want to get across with each screen shot.

◆ You should produce between 8–10 scenes.

◆ Use this activity sheet and Activity Sheet 5.10b to help you organise your ideas.

Screen 1: Screen shot

Screen 1: Voice over

Screen 2: Screen shot

Screen 2: Voice over

Screen 3: Screen shot

Screen 3: Voice over

Screen 4: Screen shot

Screen 4: Voice over

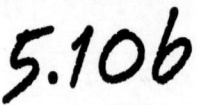

How did the world help?

Screen 5: Screen shot

Screen 5: Voice over

_____
_____
_____
_____

Screen 6: Screen shot

Screen 6: Voice over

_____
_____
_____
_____

Screen 7: Screen shot

Screen 7: Voice over

_____
_____
_____
_____

Screen 8: Screen shot

Screen 8: Voice over

_____
_____
_____
_____

Screen 9: Screen shot

Screen 9: Voice over

_____
_____
_____
_____

Screen 10: Screen shot

Screen 10: Voice over

_____
_____
_____
_____

How can the tsunami danger be reduced?

Many people live in areas of the world that may be affected by natural disasters. MEDCs are often able to cope a little better with these disasters than LEDCs. However, it is a struggle for all people and places affected to get back to 'normality' and the routine of life after a catastrophic event.

1 Read the statements below. Using a **red** pencil for MEDCs and a **green** pencil for LEDCs, carefully colour code the statements correctly. Be careful, you may have to use both colours for some of the statements!

Local services, e.g. fire, police and ambulance, are well trained to cope with disaster.

Some buildings are tsunami-proof, but poorly built.

Hospitals are well prepared for treating victims and survivors.

Community is ready and willing to search for victims and survivors, but lacks equipment like heavy-lifting equipment.

Country looks to international aid and world charities for help.

Tsunami evacuation measures are tested regularly. People know what to do.

Roads and railways are not always built to a high standard – difficulty in reaching victims.

There is limited access to computers to help manage relief operation.

Tsunami warning centres offer an early warning system helping to inform people of likely danger.

Counselling is available for emotionally-distressed children.

Some people lack radio or TV contact which would allow time for people to evacuate danger zones.

Airfields to bring in rescue teams and emergency supplies are often many miles away.

Country has limited money to help pay for supplies and rebuilding programmes.

There are very limited supplies for a large number of victims.

 2 Using the information above, explain why the Indian Ocean tsunami killed so many people.

Reducing the effects of tsunamis

Cut out the dominoes below and study the phrases written on them. Set the dominoes out in a straight line. Now arrange the dominoes in the correct order. You may only put a domino in place if you can explain to your group the link between the phrases you are putting together. There is only one correct order!

Predicting a tsunami

prediction.	Scientists use a sensitive instrument called a seismometer

affect the size and speed of the waves.	Sensors send data from the sea bed

howl.	Sri Lankan elephants and leopards

to a buoy floating out at sea.	The buoy then sends data to a

START	The first method that can be used to reduce the effects of a tsunami is

crawl out of their holes.	Dogs

satellite.	When information is received by the tsunami centre from the satellite

it issues alert warnings.	The fact that scientists can predict a tsunami is important

were reported dead after the Asian tsunami.	FINISH

to measure shockwaves.	The size of the shockwaves

Pacific Ocean has been successful for years.	Scientists are not the only ones who

time to prepare for a disaster.	The early warning system in the

can predict a tsunami.	Animals like snakes and rats

because it gives people	and emergency services

were seen to leave the danger area.	Few animals

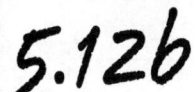

Reducing the effects of tsunamis

Preparing for a tsunami

disaster plan.	A good disaster plan will

preparation.	This is where you prepare

avoid the huge waves.	A young British girl in Thailand saved

local people	and the emergency services

so that they are ready for a disaster.	Most countries prepare by writing a

time to escape.	FINISH

They can then	run for high ground and

START	The second method that can be used to reduce the effects of a tsunami is

involve local authorities,	emergency services and

flooding.	The best way to stop this is to

educate people	about the signs of a tsunami.

local people in the area.	Most deaths are caused by

receded.	She warned people on the beach and gave them

100s of people	by noticing that the sea had

Reducing the effects of tsunamis

Use the questions below to reflect on the information you have organised in your dominoes on Activity Sheets 5.12a and b. In your group, present your findings to the rest of the class. Write down your answers below to prepare you for your presentation.

Can you identify the method used to reduce the effects of a tsunami?

The method of management we looked at was... _____

_____

List the strategies used in this method to reduce the effects and save lives.

The strategies used to predict/prepare might be... _____

_____

_____

_____

Select the strategy you think would save the most lives. Explain why.

We think that... _____

_____

_____

_____

Name as many organisations/groups of people who would be responsible for this type of disaster management.

Scientists are important because they... _____

_____

_____

_____

The tsunami enquiry

Evaluating the strengths and weaknesses of the different tsunami management schemes

◆ Use the table below to help you consider which of the management schemes on page 101 in the pupil book would help you to fulfil the different aims of the Disaster Emergency Agency.

◆ For each of the schemes, think carefully about which of the four aims the scheme would help. Put a tick in the appropriate box if the scheme does help fulfil the aim.

◆ At the end of this task you should be able to see clearly which schemes will help you to achieve which of your aims.

Aim	Feeding scheme	Home building scheme	Job provision	Medical aid scheme	Building equipment	Shelter and warmth	Hospital reconstruction	Emergency warning system
1 To provide immediate help and save lives.								
2 To care for those in need and provide long-term support.								
3 To support appropriate and sustainable long-term solutions to local problems.								
4 To support projects that enable local people to help themselves.								

The tsunami enquiry

Checklist ✓

Use the Checklist below to help you to complete your enquiry successfully. You should include all of the *should* sections. If you wish to improve your work you should include the *could* suggestions.

Section 1 — Introduction

Student Assessor

You should...

- describe where the project area of Galle is ☐ ☐
- summarise the events that have taken place in Galle ☐ ☐
- use facts and figures to describe the damage that has been done. ☐ ☐

You could...

- use an annotated sketch map to show the location of the project area ☐ ☐
- use quotes to highlight the damage done and the effects on people's lives. ☐ ☐

Section 2 — Main section

You should...

- include a table like that on page 100 in the pupil book ☐ ☐
- include a ranked list of schemes in your table that you want to use in Galle ☐ ☐
- show the cost of each scheme and the overall cost in your table ☐ ☐
- list the schemes you would use to provide immediate help to the people of Galle ☐ ☐
- state how each scheme will help tackle a specific local problem ☐ ☐
- list the schemes you would use to help the people of Galle help themselves and for the recovery to be sustainable (long-term) ☐ ☐
- for each scheme, state how local people will be involved and what local problem the scheme would help solve ☐ ☐
- list the schemes you would use to reduce the effect of a future tsunami in Galle ☐ ☐
- explain how this scheme would reduce the amount of damage done to Galle. ☐ ☐

You could...

- have a further four columns, one for each of the aims of the Disaster Emergency Agency ☐ ☐
- add a tick to each column if the aims are fulfilled by each different scheme you have chosen ☐ ☐
- include facts to show how big the present problem is ☐ ☐
- include facts/examples of the present damage that could be prevented. ☐ ☐

Section 3 — Conclusion

You should...

- summarise which of the projects you would recommend spending the £500,000 on. ☐ ☐

You could...

- give some indication of what time periods you would suggest implementing the different schemes. ☐ ☐

Think about your learning!

Before you submit your final enquiry, spend some time thinking about the learning that you have carried out.

1 Look carefully at this list of skills. Geographers are skilled people! **Tick** the skills you are developing during your time working on this enquiry.

2 Describe **one** thing that enabled you to be successful in this task:

_____

_____

_____

_____

3 Describe **one** problem you had, or thought you had, that stopped you from achieving your potential:

_____

_____

_____

_____

_____

Teamwork	☐
Reading	☐
Listening	☐
Discussion	☐
Problem solving	☐
Decision making	☐
Map interpretation	☐
Graphing	☐
Data analysis	☐
Questioning	☐
Debating	☐
Time management	☐
Presenting	☐
Empathy	☐
Annotation	☐
Evaluation	☐
Research	☐
Using ICT	☐
Comparing	☐

4 In these boxes write **two** actions that you will carry out to help you be more successful and reach your target in the future.

 **The United Kingdom**   *Unit Overview*

Approximate teaching time, 14 hours

KEY IDEAS:

◆ the UK's physical and human geography
◆ where people in the UK come from

◆ the UK's wealth and regional differences
◆ describing the local area.

Pos	Key questions	Pupil book	Suggested activities/methods
3a	What is the UK like?	102, 103	Pupils could compile a list of what they see as characteristic features of the United Kingdom.
3a	Where is the UK?	104	The UK can be located with reference to the continents and oceans.
3c	What is the UK?	105	The technique of classification can be explained with reference to its uses in this book. The technique can then be applied to the countries of the British Isles.
3c	What are the UK's main physical features?	106, 107	Photos of physical features and weather are described then located on maps of the UK's climate. The UK is divided into climate sectors, based on temperature and rainfall.
3c	How is the UK divided up?	108, 109	Division of the UK into different administrative units. Discussion of pupils' home addresses and locations within this framework.
3c, 3d, 3e, 4b	Where do people in the UK come from?	110, 111	Learn the terms connected with migration. Carry out a class survey of birth place and migration history. Display and analyse the results.
4b	How well off is the UK?	112, 113	Discuss the classification of employment types. Analyse the regional distribution of income in the UK.
6a, 3a	What are the regional differences in the UK?	114, 115	Synthesise information from the whole unit on relief, climate, settlement and economic activities to produce geography FactFiles for six regions of the UK.
2b	What is it like where you live?	118, 119	Using environmental surveys to assess quality of life in a local area.
2d	How can the internet be used in a geographical enquiry?	120, 121	Using internet sources, for example Multimap, to research information about a local area.
3a, 3b, 3c, 1a–f	The UK enquiry – what are some of England's most interesting places?	122, 123	Research a variety of places using book and/or ICT resources then produce an illustrated diary or plan for a tour of England with a foreign friend.

PoS	Skills
1a–f	Enquiry skills
1c	Selecting relevant graphs and drawing them
1d	Synthesising data from various sources
2b	Questionnaire survey
2c	Use of atlas
2d	Classification
2d	Photo analysis
2d	Analysis of paintings

Vocabulary and technical terms

(see Glossary in pupil book)

Climate	Map	Refugees
Drought	Migration	Satellite image
Economic geography	Multicultural society	Secondary activities
Emigrant	Ordnance Survey	Service activities
Ethnic groups	Physical geography	Standard of living
European Union	Population	Temperature
Hazard	Precipitation	Tertiary activities
Immigrant	Primary activities	Urban
Land use	Quality of life	

Assessment for Learning

Pages 110–111: Activity Sheet 6.7

Pupils should be encouraged to discuss their thoughts on push and pull factors. This discussion will help pupils to clarify their understanding.

Once the activity is complete, use the following questions to draw out pupils' understanding:

◆ What push and pull factors do you think are important in influencing the movement of people in or out of our local area?

◆ Which push and pull factors do you think are the most influential in our local area?

◆ Which cartoon do you think best reflects how the population is changing in our area?

◆ What evidence have you seen in the area to suggest that this is the case?

◆ What are the benefits of new people moving in to create a multicultural society?

◆ Why might people moving out be a problem?

Once the question and answers are complete, give pupils time to develop their work based on the new ideas and learning.

Differentiation
To simplify the activity sheet, cut off the lower part and ask pupils to work in pairs from the beginning.

Extension
Ask extension pupils to choose a different region in the UK where they think the situation might be different. It may be a place they have visited in the UK. Alternatively, you may choose to provide an image of an area that pupils can use as a prompt.

Pages 112–113: Activity Sheet 6.11

Before the activity begins, make a list of information that you are expecting pupils to include in their answers. Each piece of information should be assigned a score depending on how difficult it is to find in the pupil book. This should be written on an OHT or flipchart so it can be displayed at the front of the class. Once pupils have answered the first question, share your information with the class and pupils can mark their own or a partner's work to see how many points they have accrued. Pupils should make a list of the information that they have missed underneath their work.

Differentiation
Pupils may need an explanation of 'quality of life'. Link it to the characteristics they have picked out in answering question 1.

Extension
Ask pupils to make a list of additional information (primary or secondary) that they would need to make a more detailed assessment of the wealth of Britain and how it changes over time. Who would they need to contact for this information?

Pages 114–115: Activity Sheet 6.12

Before this task, discuss with pupils what kinds of information you would expect to see included in the Venn diagram. Examples would include climate, population density and types of industry.

Differentiation
Nominate a region to compare the pupils' home region with. Give pupils nine pieces of information for them to sort into the correct sections of the Venn diagram.

Extension
Pupils should be asked to predict how their region might change in the next 50 years.

Pages 104–109, 114–115, 118–121: Activity Sheet 6.14

This activity is designed to draw together a number of themes that pupils will have learned about. It can be used in conjunction with Activity Sheets 6.3a and b.

Assessment for Learning
By providing pupils with success criteria, they are more likely to achieve a desirable end result. It is important to give pupils time to reflect on the success criteria so that they are clear about what they will need to do to. The activity can be followed up by asking pupils to peer assess each other's work using the success criteria as a guide to marking. Allocate more time to allow the pupils to edit their answers in the light of the peer assessment.

Differentiation
Reduce the number of success criteria or ask pupils to choose only three of the criteria.

Extension
Encourage pupils to include some original ideas in their work. This ensures that, although they work to success criteria, their imagination and creativity is not stifled.

Pages 122–123: The UK enquiry

The UK enquiry Checklist (page 175) can be used in three ways.

1 Firstly, the pupils need to complete the Checklist. This ensures they think about what information needs to be included and where that information may come from.

2 After the enquiry has been completed, the Checklist can be used by pupils to check whether or not they have met the success criteria for the enquiry. As they complete each task, pupils can tick the parts they have completed. If there are any parts not ticked, pupils can be sure of what they need to include to complete the enquiry.

3 The Checklist can also be used by an assessor (either a teacher or another pupil if an element of peer marking is to be introduced) to mark pupils' work. Once again, the boxes that remain empty will diagnose where the pupil has failed to meet the criteria. The work could be returned to the pupil once an assessor has looked at the work so that any omissions can be corrected by the pupil. This process of drafting work is an important skill for geographers and will breed good habits for future years.

The Think about your learning! assessment sheet (page 176) provides an opportunity for pupils to reflect on the work they have undertaken during the enquiry. By considering how they approached a task, pupils can compile a list of their own success criteria and analyse barriers to their learning. This information will leave them better prepared to approach the enquiry in other units.

What is the UK like?

 Read the questions below and decide where each question fits around the development compass.

 Write the questions in one of the four spaces around the development compass.

 Use these questions to ask about the different pictures and photos in this unit. Try to answer the questions for the places in each image.

What is the climate like here?
Who designed this building?
How crowded is it here?
What is the environment like?
How good is the quality of life?
How rich or poor are people here?
What are the buildings used for?
Who designed this place?

How is the land used?
Why do people live here?
What jobs do people do?
How safe is it to live here?
What improvements might people want?
What natural vegetation grows here?
What are the buildings made of?
To what extent do people have choices about their lives?

Nature and the environment

_____
_____
_____
_____

Who decides and choices for possible futures

_____
_____
_____
_____

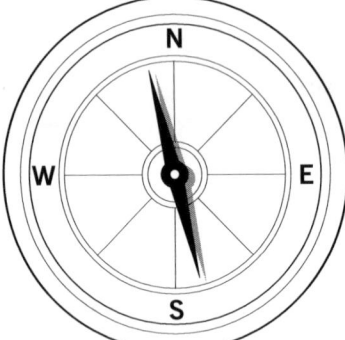

Economic and trade issues

_____
_____
_____
_____

Social issues and the people

_____
_____
_____
_____

 Study the list below of where we get our images. Make a list of the type of images you get of the UK from:

TV   Books   Comics   Videos/films   Newspapers   Charities
School subjects   Advertisements   Other

What is your home town or city like?

Geography is about people and places. Think about your home town or city. Imagine that you have a new pen-pal who lives in the USA. You decide to send a postcard to tell this friend all about your home town. Find out information from books, the school library, Tourist Information and the internet – use a search engine and simply type in the name of your home town or city.

Decide on the best image for your home town. Paste or draw it below and then complete your postcard.

How might we promote the UK?

Imagine that you work for a travel agent called *Get Away!* The company wants to promote the UK across Europe. Your job is to outline the introduction to a short DVD that *Get Away!* will use to promote holidays in the UK.

Working with a partner or in a small group, you will need to:

◆ write the script and draw a storyboard

◆ think carefully about its content – what main attractions does the UK have to offer?

◆ think carefully about the screen shots you want to use. You could glue photos into the storyboard or draw pictures, or even write short descriptions of what you would show.

◆ include a voice over for each frame. Think carefully about the message you want to get across with each screen shot.

◆ produce between 8–10 scenes.

Use this activity sheet and Activity Sheet 6.3b to help you organise your ideas.

Screen 1: Screen shot

Screen 1: Voice over

_____

_____

_____

_____

Screen 2: Screen shot

Screen 2: Voice over

_____

_____

_____

_____

Screen 3: Screen shot

Screen 3: Voice over

_____

_____

_____

_____

Screen 4: Screen shot

Screen 4: Voice over

_____

_____

_____

_____

How might we promote the UK?

Screen 5: Screen shot

Screen 5: Voice over

_____

_____

_____

_____

Screen 6: Screen shot

Screen 6: Voice over

_____

_____

_____

_____

Screen 7: Screen shot

Screen 7: Voice over

_____

_____

_____

_____

Screen 8: Screen shot

Screen 8: Voice over

_____

_____

_____

_____

Screen 9: Screen shot

Screen 9: Voice over

_____

_____

_____

_____

Screen 10: Screen shot

Screen 10: Voice over

_____

_____

_____

_____

What are the UK's main physical and human features?

Both the scenery and climate of the UK are varied. Usually the scenery is very attractive while the climate is temperate. Most people in the UK live in England. The UK can be subdivided into countries, economic and administrative regions.

Below is a list of words to do with the UK.

1	England.	**14**	Scotland.	**27**	Regions.
2	Hilly.	**15**	Relief.	**28**	Opinions.
3	Weather.	**16**	Lake District.	**29**	Flat.
4	Perceptions.	**17**	Dartmoor.	**30**	Lowland.
5	Locations.	**18**	Stereotype.	**31**	Grampian Mountains.
6	The Fens.	**19**	Destinations.	**32**	Edinburgh.
7	The Pennines.	**20**	Wales.	**33**	Cardiff.
8	Republic of Ireland.	**21**	Facts.	**34**	London.
9	Images.	**22**	Identity.	**35**	Northern Ireland.
10	Wind.	**23**	Great Britain.	**36**	United Kingdom.
11	Climate.	**24**	Forecast.	**37**	British Isles.
12	Rainfall.	**25**	Temperature.	**38**	Belfast.
13	Temperate.	**26**	Places.		

a Working with a partner, study the sets of numbers below, which match to words in the list above.

b Cross out the 'odd one out' in each set.

c Add a fourth number to match the other two.

d Explain what links the three 'in' numbers.

Set A	1	14	32	
What's the link?				
Set B	16	7	6	
What's the link?				
Set C	2	25	12	
What's the link?				
Set D	5	26	14	
What's the link?				
Set E	9	4	24	
What's the link?				
Set F	33	38	27	
What's the link?				

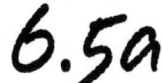

Where do people in the UK come from?

Migration is the movement of people from one place to another to live or to work. International and internal migration may be forced or voluntary. Forced migration happens when people have no choice but to move. They are forced out by push factors. When people choose to move, because of pull factors elsewhere, that is voluntary migration.

Below is a list of words to do with migration.

1　Commuting to and from work each day.

2　Wars creating large numbers of refugees.

3　Leaving to live in Spain for three years.

4　Moving to avoid natural disasters such as volcanic eruptions.

5　National service.

6　Moving to find better housing.

7　Refugee.

8　Racial discrimination.

9　Moving to live in a cleaner, safer environment.

10　Going to work in London for six months.

11　Free health care.

12　Asylum seeker.

13　Immigration.

14　Losing your job.

15　Moving to escape from poverty on poor farmland.

16　Moving to improve standard of living.

17　Moving to avoid crime.

18　Emigration.

19　Moving to be with friends and relatives.

20　Moving to live in a better climate, especially in retirement.

21　Migration.

22　Freedom of speech.

23　Moving to escape religious or political persecution.

24　Moving to improve quality of life.

25　Economic migrant.

26　Going shopping for the day.

27　Moving to an area with cheaper house prices.

28　Flying to Paris for a one-day business meeting.

29　Retiring to the coast from life in the city.

30　Better services such as hospitals, schools and entertainment.

31　Moving because of a lack of food due to crop failure.

32　Leaving after 10 years of drought.

33　Moving to find a job or earn a higher salary.

34　Going round Europe picking grapes during the summer.

35　To escape compulsory labour like slavery.

36　Leaving to enjoy a greater chance of education.

Where do people in the UK come from?

 a Study the sets of numbers below, which match
to words in the list on Activity Sheet 6.5a.

b Cross out the 'odd one out' in each set.

c Explain what links the two 'in' numbers.

Set A	1	10	3
What's the link?			
Set B	12	7	25
What's the link?			
Set C	22	11	5
What's the link?			
Set D	18	21	13
What's the link?			
Set E	19	4	20
What's the link?			
Set F	9	17	28
What's the link?			
Set G	26	29	28
What's the link?			
Set H	23	14	24
What's the link?			

 Highlight the statements describing causes of
voluntary migration in red, and causes of forced
migration in green.

 Complete a copy of the table below using the
statements on Activity Sheet 6.5a.

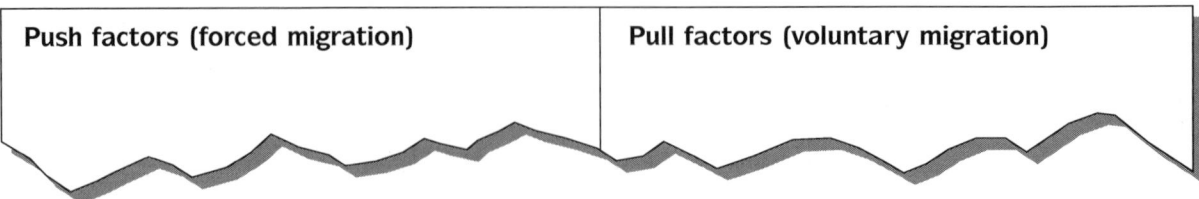

Push factors (forced migration)	Pull factors (voluntary migration)

The table only tells part of the story of why people
migrate. It is not always a simple choice. There is
a lot more to migration than push and pull!

Where do people in the UK come from?

 a Cut out the dominoes below and study the key words written on them.

    b Working in pairs, lay all the dominoes in a straight line.

    c Now arrange the dominoes in the correct order. You may only put a domino in place if you can explain to your partner the link between the words that you are putting together. There is only one correct order!

Pull factor	Leave the area

Children have to work	High birth rate

Farm sold	No job to go to

No pension	Poor health care

Arrive	New city

Few prospects	Little or no education

Crops fail again	No food to eat

No mortgage to pay	Shantytown settlement

Push factor	Better prospects in city

Travel	Migrant

Immigrant	Feel like an outsider

Poor health and illness	High infant mortality

Cannot pay the rent	No home

Few friends or family	No money

Informal job	Poor pay

 Stick the dominoes in your book or file in the correct order.

 Explain the pattern of events that may lead to the movement of people from one place to another.

Where do people come from in our local area?

1 Label your settlement on the UK map below.

2 List four pull factors under the appropriate heading. These are factors that might encourage people to move into your area.

3 List four push factors under the appropriate heading. These are factors that might encourage people to move out of your area.

4 Discuss with a partner which of the seesaws at the bottom of the page best reflects the state of the population in your area.

5 List the positives and negatives of the situation in your area.

Pull factors   **Push factors**

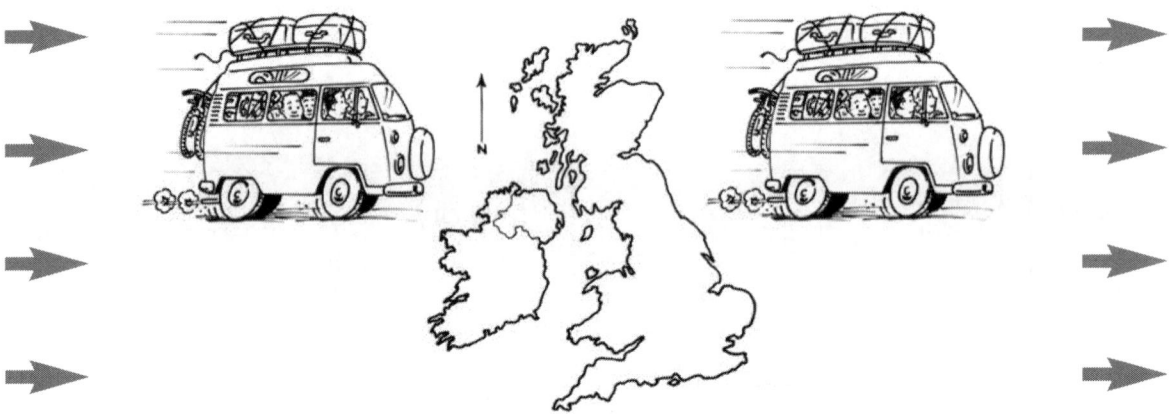

Positives   **Negatives**

People move in ———————————— People move out

People move in ———————————— People move out

People move in ———————————— People move out

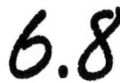

How well off is the UK?

Jobs, or economic activities, may be divided into three main groups: primary; secondary and tertiary.

Below is a list of words to do with economic activities.

1	Natural resources.	**9**	Health.	**17**	Manufacturing.
2	Tourism.	**10**	Entertainment.	**18**	Steel industry.
3	Car assembly.	**11**	Secondary activity.	**19**	Tertiary industry.
4	Education.	**12**	Fishing.	**20**	Teaching.
5	Farming.	**13**	Transport.	**21**	Bricklayer.
6	Retailing.	**14**	Building new houses.	**22**	Nurse.
7	Forestry.	**15**	Primary activity.		
8	Service activities.	**16**	Mining and quarrying.		

 1 a Working with a partner, study the sets of numbers below, which match to words in the list above.

b Cross out the 'odd one out' in each set.

c Add a fourth number to match the other two.

d Explain what links the three 'in' numbers.

Set A	5	20	12	
What's the link?				
Set B	2	10	7	
What's the link?				
Set C	4	7	9	
What's the link?				
Set D	1	4	16	
What's the link?				
Set E	17	6	14	
What's the link?				
Set F	3	2	11	
What's the link?				
Set G	13	8	19	
What's the link?				

How does the standard of living differ in the UK?

The UK can be divided into several regions. Development is not spread evenly. Some people in the UK still have a poor standard of living.

Below are two sets of cards showing:

◆ UK average weekly pay

◆ UK average unemployment.

1 Cut out the cards and stick them near each correct region on the map on Activity Sheet 6.9b.

2 Working with a partner, what evidence can you find between the standard of living in the north and south? You may also use map **D** on page 113 in the pupil book to help you. Be sure to give reasons for your answer.

UK average weekly pay

Scotland £440	Yorkshire and the Humber £425	East Midlands £430
North West £440	East £475	Wales £41
West Midlands £435	South West £440	South East £500
Northern Ireland £400	North East £400	

UK average unemployment

Scotland 7.5%	Yorkshire and the Humber 6%	East Midlands 5%
North West 5%	East 3.5%	Wales 6%
West Midlands 6%	South West 4%	South East 3%
Northern Ireland 7%	North East 9%	

168

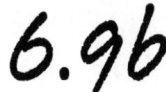

How does the standard of living differ in the UK?

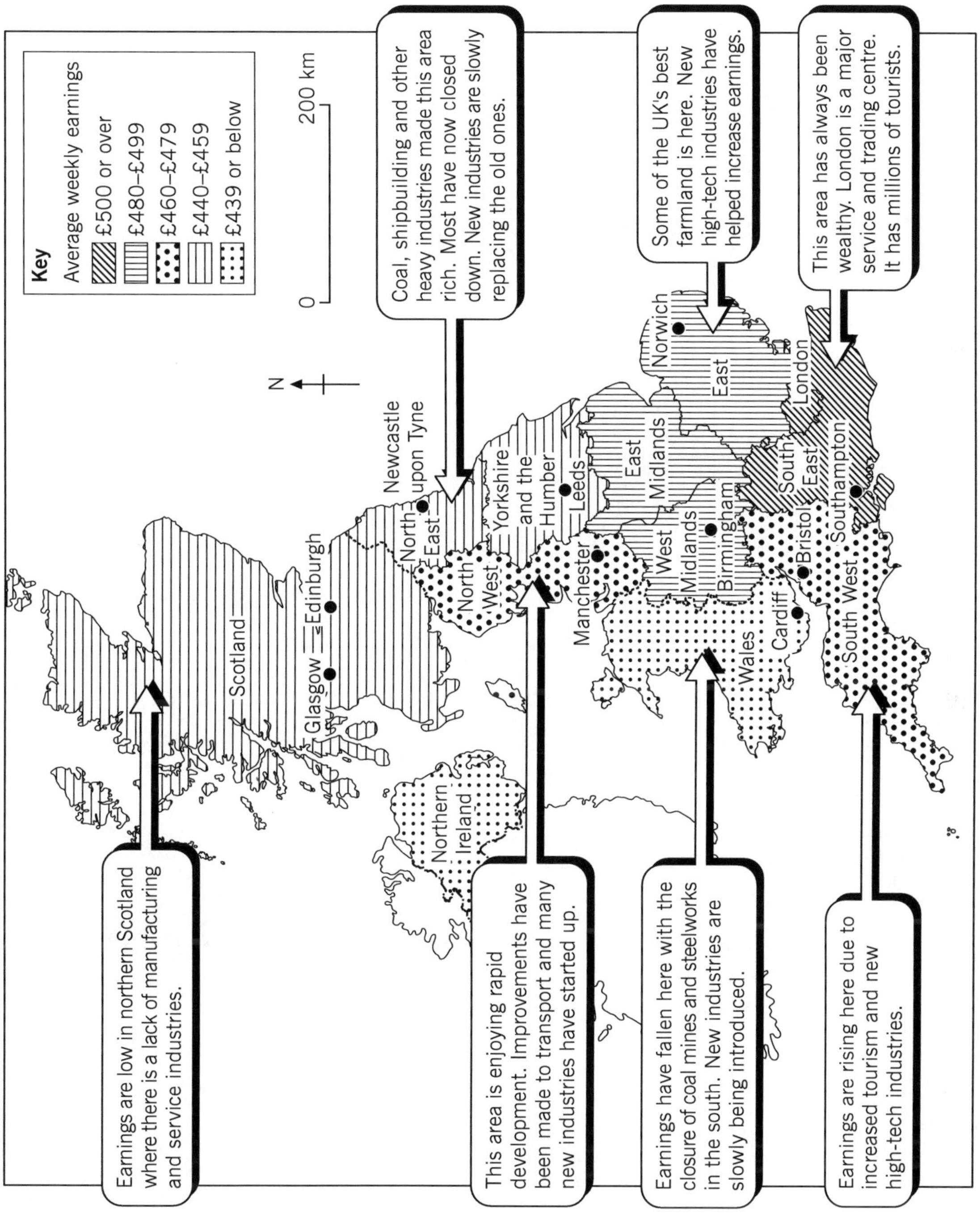

Key

Average weekly earnings

- £500 or over
- £480–£499
- £460–£479
- £440–£459
- £439 or below

0   200 km

N

Scotland

Glasgow
Edinburgh

Newcastle
upon Tyne

North
East

North
West

Yorkshire
and the
Humber

Leeds

Manchester

Northern
Ireland

Wales

Cardiff

West
Midlands

East
Midlands

Birmingham

East

Norwich

London

South
East

South West

Bristol

Southampton

Coal, shipbuilding and other heavy industries made this area rich. Most have now closed down. New industries are slowly replacing the old ones.

Some of the UK's best farmland is here. New high-tech industries have helped increase earnings.

This area has always been wealthy. London is a major service and trading centre. It has millions of tourists.

Earnings are low in northern Scotland where there is a lack of manufacturing and service industries.

This area is enjoying rapid development. Improvements have been made to transport and many new industries have started up.

Earnings have fallen here with the closure of coal mines and steelworks in the south. New industries are slowly being introduced.

Earnings are rising here due to increased tourism and new high-tech industries.

How developed is the UK?

The UK is one of the most developed countries in the world. Development is not spread evenly. Some people in the UK still have a poor standard of living.

 1 Working with a partner, read and cut out the following development indicators, which can be used to measure development.

Crime	Concern for the environment	Air quality
Shopper goods	Clean water	Cities
Freedom and democracy	Jobs	Peace
Trade	Equality	Power supply
Quality housing	Wealth	Health
Strong defence	Transport	Modern industry
Education	Women's rights	Sufficient food
Access to technology		

2 Select nine development indicators that you think are the most important and arrange these statements into an order of importance in the diamond arrangement shown on the right.

3 Explain your choice for the most important development indicator.

4 Think about the area where you live. Use the development indicators above and make a list to explain how your area is developed.

5 Do you think that all areas of the UK are developed? Give reasons for your answer.

Most important

1

2   2

3   3   3

2   2

1

Least important

How well off is your home region?

1 Collect as much information as you can about the
state of wealth in your home region. Use pages 112
and 113 in the pupil book to help you.

_____

_____

_____

_____

_____

_____

_____

_____

_____

_____

2 Describe ways in which you think this might affect
the quality of life in your region.

_____

_____

_____

_____

_____

_____

_____

_____

_____

_____

_____

3 Name a region that has greater wealth than
your home region.

_____

4 Name a region that has less wealth than your
home region.

_____

What are the regional differences in the UK?

You are going to compare your region with another region in the UK.

Using pages 114 and 115 in the pupil book, complete the Venn diagram below.
If there is any information that applies to both regions, write it where the two
circles overlap.

Your home region

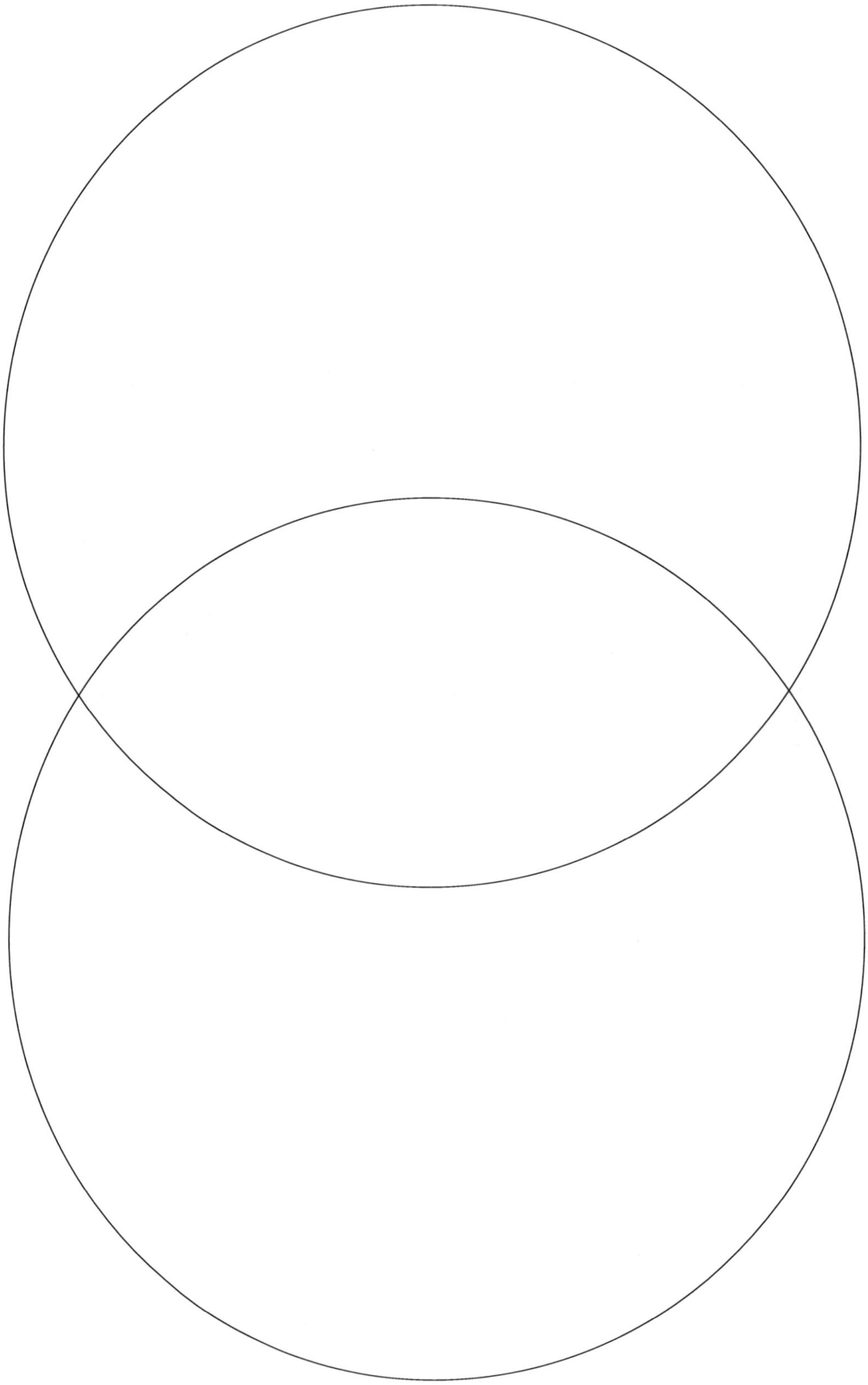

What is it like where you live?

Most of us live in a neighbourhood. This is the area that immediately surrounds the building in which we live. It could be a few streets that make up part of a town or city, or it could be the whole of a small town or village.

 1 Look carefully at photos **A** and **B** showing two different types of environment in the UK on page 118 in the pupil book. In which photo are you most likely to come across the following things? Enter A or B in the left-hand columns of the table below.

Photo		Photo	
	Noisy neighbours.		Houses with burglar alarms and window locks.
	Reduced pollution and a cleaner environment.		The most expensive land.
	Derelict buildings and disused factories.		A good community feeling.
	Town centre redevelopment.		Children playing outside in the street.
	Garages and 'lock-ups'.		Old buildings being demolished.
	A corner shop open late at night.		Cars speeding.
	Litter and graffiti.		Houses in need of repair.
	Old people and families with young children.		The air polluted by harmful exhaust fumes.
	Crowds and busy streets.		A cycle path.
	Vandalism, litter and crime.		Improved local shopping facilities.
	A new supermarket opening soon.		Your car stolen.
	Restaurants, cafés, museums, cinemas and entertainment.		Open space and greenery.
	High-rise flats.		Children playing safely in the street.
	New shopping centre.		Difficulty parking your car.
	Boarded-up empty homes in need of renovation.		A bus service into town.
	Pensioners who've lived in the same house all their lives.		A better quality of life.

 2 Explain why photo **A** shows a better environment than photo **B**.

 3 Using your local newspaper, find adverts for property or houses for sale in your neighbourhood. Cut out the adverts, then label and stick them in your book or file. Use all that you have learned from this exercise to label the adverts and add other labels of your own.

Remember: Be careful when you are working with different viewpoints. Are your answers based on real knowledge or are they based on stereotypes and prejudice?

 4 Imagine that your home is for sale. How would you sell your home to a buyer? Write the advert for an estate agent.

The creative challenge

◆ Design a DVD for a travel agent called *Get Away!*
◆ The aim of the DVD is to promote the UK as a European holiday destination.

A successful DVD will fulfil the following product and content criteria:

Product criteria

You will produce either a storyboard or a PowerPoint presentation.
It needs to be:

◆ exciting and engaging
◆ persuasive enough to convince people to visit the UK for their next holiday.

Content criteria

Your presentation will contain:

◆ eye-catching images that highlight the diversity and interest of the UK as a place to visit
◆ informative text that can be read or added as a voice over to your presentation
◆ facts about famous places in the UK
◆ lots of examples of places of interest
◆ lots of ideas, for example: where people should go; what they might do; how long they will spend there.

The presentation will contain information about:

◆ where the UK is in Europe: location maps; transport connections; journey times ☐
◆ the UK's physical features: regional differences and common characteristics ☐
◆ climate: the weather visitors should expect as they travel around the UK ☐
◆ some of the main human attractions: buildings; museums; visitor attractions ☐
◆ some of the main physical attractions: famous natural landmarks and activities to take part in ☐
◆ two-day trips in two contrasting regions (you may include your own home region) ☐
◆ internet sites readers could use to research and plan their trip to the UK in more detail. ☐

Resources you can use

Use the information you have learned in class but also feel free to use your own personal experience of places you have visited on holiday or visiting relatives.

You can interview relatives and friends who live in different areas of the UK to you. They might even send you pictures of the place they live or leaflets from their local tourist information centre.

You can carry out additional research using the internet, holiday brochures or your local tourist information centre.

Checklist ✓

To help you complete your enquiry successfully, you need to think about your work before you begin. This activity sheet will help you.

1 Make a list of what an excellent sightseeing tour will include.

2 Use the bullet points below to record all the things you will need to plan your tour (think about distances, journey times and the places your pen-pal might want to visit).

- _____ ☐
- _____ ☐
- _____ ☐
- _____ ☐
- _____ ☐

3 Complete a copy of the spider diagram below by listing where you will look for the information to help you complete your enquiry.

Where might you look to find this information?

Who might you ask?

4 Make a large copy of the table on page 123 in the pupil book. Use this to plan your sightseeing tour in rough.

5 Make a list of things you would need to check before you complete your plan. The first one has been completed for you.

- The number of days the tour will last. _____ ☐
- _____ ☐
- _____ ☐
- _____ ☐
- _____ ☐

6 Once you are confident that your plan will work, it is time to write up your final seven-day sightseeing tour of England and Wales. Make a list of what you need to do. Put a number by each task to show the order you are going to complete them in. Good luck!

> Once you have completed your enquiry, but before you hand it in, go through the checklist above again to check that you have completed all of the correct sections. You can tick the boxes so that you know what you have included.

Think about your learning!

Before you submit your final enquiry, spend some time thinking about the learning that you have carried out.

Teamwork	☐
Reading	☐
Listening	☐
Discussion	☐
Problem solving	☐
Decision making	☐
Map interpretation	☐
Graphing	☐
Data analysis	☐
Questioning	☐
Debating	☐
Time management	☐
Presenting	☐
Empathy	☐
Annotation	☐
Evaluation	☐
Research	☐
Using ICT	☐
Comparing	☐

1 Look carefully at this list of skills. Geographers are skilled people! **Tick** the skills you are developing during your time working on this enquiry.

2 Describe **one** thing that enabled you to be successful in this task:

_____

_____

_____

_____

3 Describe **one** problem you had, or thought you had, that stopped you from achieving your potential:

_____

_____

_____

_____

4 In these boxes write **two** actions that you will carry out to help you be more successful and reach your target in the future.

7 Map skills

Approximate teaching time, 14 hours

KEY IDEAS:

◆ how to work out distance and direction
◆ how to use map symbols
◆ how to use four and six figure map references

◆ how height and shape of the land are shown on a map
◆ how to plan and follow routes on a map.

Pos	Key questions	Pupil book	Suggested activities/methods
2c	How can we use maps?	124, 125	Discuss with pupils where they encounter maps in their lives, and in what circumstances they may be used.
2c	How can the eight points of the compass be used to show direction?	126, 127	Define what maps and plans are. Describe different types of map and their uses. Draw an eight-point compass for a wall display. Give directions around the classroom.
2c, 2e	How can straight line distances be measured on a map or plan? How can scale be used to find real distances on a map or plan?	128, 129	Look at different scale lines in an atlas. Measure distance on a school plan. Play the Treasure Hunt game – distance and direction. Draw a plan of the classroom to scale.
2c, 2e	How can symbols be used to show map features? How are symbols used on an OS map?	130, 131	Invent symbols for common features – TV, car, etc. Draw map of local street using symbols. Sort OS symbols into four types. Draw map of imaginary island using OS symbols.
2c	How can four figure grid references be used to locate features on a map?	132, 133	Draw grid on school plan and give references. Give grid references from local OS map.
2c, 2e	How can six figure grid references be used to locate features on a map?	134, 135	Pupils to design instructions for teaching young children six figure grid references. Follow a route using six figure grid references on a local area OS map.
2c, 2e	What methods can be used to show height and relief on a map?	136–139	Define methods and terms. Study relief map of Britain. Colour in relief map of local area. Name features. Complete unfinished contour map and convert to layer colouring.
2c, 2e	How can a route be followed on a map? How can an OS map be used to describe the landscape? How can maps be used to plan routes and measure distances?	140, 141	Describe the route from home to school. Describe and follow a route on the school plan. Give directions from school to a nearby feature using an OS map. Describe a village/beauty spot from an OS map.

PoS	Skills
2c	Locate a place on a map
2e	Map a route using symbols

Vocabulary and technical terms

(see Glossary in pupil book)

Contour	Ordnance Survey
Contour interval	Plan
Direction	Points of the compass
Four figure grid reference	Relief
Grid square	Scale
Height	Six figure grid reference
Key	Spot height
Layer colouring	Symbol
Map	Triangulation pillar

Assessment for Learning

No activity sheets have been provided for Unit 7 as it is a skills-based unit. Instead, guidance is given below to enhance particular activities in the pupil book.

Throughout the map skills unit there are opportunities for self and peer assessment. Most of the activities ask for answers which are correct or incorrect. Teachers can go through the answers to the activities as a whole class whilst pupils mark and correct their own work, or pupils can swap books and their work can be peer assessed. It is important that time is allowed for pupils to correct their work by attempting the questions again.

To introduce an element of coaching, pairs of pupils should be given an answer sheet and as they mark each other's work should pick out incorrect answers and coach each other towards the correct answer.

Pages 140–141

Activity 2b on page 141 of the pupil book asks pupils to write a description of the village of Newton and the surrounding area to advertise a holiday cottage. This provides an opportunity for pupils to draft work before it is submitted. Once pupils have written their description, it should be read over by two other pupils and constructive criticism given. This provides guidance as to how to improve, as well as meaning that all pupils will have seen another example of the work from which they can take ideas.

Map skills Checklist

The map skills Checklist (page 191) is designed to help pupils and teachers assess the level of understanding of each topic in the unit. After each topic is studied, pupils should be asked to assess their level of understanding. If they are confident with the topic, they can highlight the smiley face. If they are not so confident, they should highlight one of the other faces. In the third column, pupils should write an important point to remember (if they are confident with the topic), e.g.: 'Always remember to go along the corridor and up the stairs'. Alternatively, if they are not so confident, pupils can write down one of the things they are struggling with. This gives them and their teacher an idea of what aspect of the topic they need to revise. The fourth column gives teachers a chance to assess the level of understanding of the pupil. If there is disagreement between the pupil and teacher over how well they understand a particular topic, then this highlights that mismatch and gives, therefore, a point for discussion.

Pupils are expected to assess their own performance by deciding how well they understand the topic in question. As map skills is often the basis for the first lessons pupils undertake at a new school, it also means that they are introduced to the idea of being responsible for assessing their own learning at an early stage in their school career.

Differentiation

Pupils who are less confident about assessing their own ability may find this task difficult. Teachers can work through the sheet with them agreeing what the pupil should write in the third column.

Extension

To check the accuracy of the self assessment, pupils could test each other and complete the teacher assessment column accordingly. This introduces an element of peer assessment.

The Think about your learning! assessment sheet (page 192) provides an opportunity for pupils to reflect on the work they have undertaken during this unit. By considering how they approached a task, pupils can compile a list of their own success criteria and analyse barriers to their learning. This information will leave them better prepared to approach other units.

How can we use maps?

Geography can be very useful to you as you start a new term in a brand-new school.

Coming to a new secondary school can be a daunting experience. Secondary schools are usually much bigger than primary schools – you may already have had difficulties finding your way around new corridors and new classrooms. I bet everybody took a wrong turn somewhere! Geography can help with this.

The map below shows a plan of your school.

Look carefully and you will see all the classrooms and their room numbers marked on the map. Working with a partner, complete the following activities.

 Use a colour code for each school subject and colour in each subject classroom.
Clue: Subject classrooms are usually grouped together.

 Carefully draw a black border around each classroom where you have lessons.
Clue: Your new timetable will show all your lessons and classrooms.

 Use your school map to plan your route to each of your lessons.

Once you've followed your new timetable for a few weeks, you may begin to remember where and when to go to your lessons. But don't throw your map away; look after it. This is one map that you could be using every day at school!

How can we show direction?

Maps are a good way of giving information and showing where places are. Direction can be described by using points of the compass.

There are four main directions. These are: north; south; east; and west. Between these there are four other directions: north-east; north-west; south-east; and south-west.

These directions are shown on this compass.

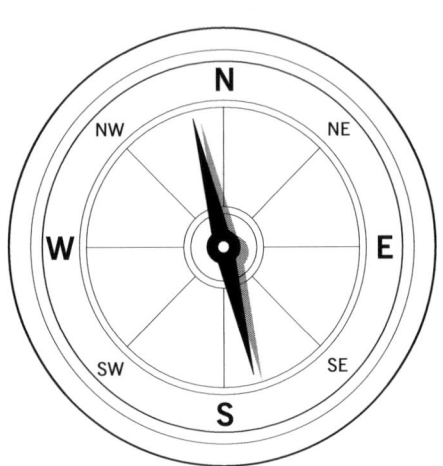

Working with a partner, practise these directions by playing the game below. You will need two dice to play.

- ◆ One player chooses the red 'start' and the other player the green 'start'.
- ◆ The winner is the first one to get to the same coloured 'finish' square.
- ◆ Throw the two dice, add up the scores and move your counter one space in the direction shown in the key below.
- ◆ Colour this square red or green.
- ◆ Be careful! You must not use a square already used by your opponent.
- ◆ If you make a mistake and your move takes you off the board, you must go back to your 'start'.

Key

Dice score	Direction
2	Any direction
3	South-east
4	North-east
5	West
6	South
7	Stay where you are!
8	East
9	North
10	South-west
11	North-west
12	Any direction

Red start								Green finish
Green start								Red finish

How can we measure distance?

Distances on a map can be measured using the scale line. The scale line gives the real distance between places on a map.

Imagine that it is the summer holidays and you are walking along the beach. You find a message in a bottle washed up by the tide. Inside, you discover a map and some kind of instructions giving you the exact location of a desert island with buried treasure! Mark on the map a good spot where the treasure might have been buried.

Just as you work out where the treasure is buried, a strong gust of wind tears the instructions from your grip leaving you only the first instruction. Quickly, and before you forget, you write down the instructions.

Start at the shipwreck and complete the set of instructions below. Ask your partner to find the booty!

Leave the wreck and go east for 2 km.
Go north for 2 km,

How do we use map symbols?

Symbols are simple drawings that show things on a map. All maps have a key to explain the symbols.

 Follow the instructions below to draw a sketch map of Keysville (a fictional village) in the grid.

 Design a symbol for each feature in the village and produce a key.

Instructions

Houses	Fill the squares 6N, 7M, 7L, 7I, 10I, 6H and 8H.
Roads	A main road runs in a straight line from 1J to 19J.
	A minor road runs in a straight line from 9A to 9O.
	A track runs in a straight line from 16C to 16J.
River	Flows in a straight line from 5A to 19L.
Pond	In square 4E.
Railway line	Runs in a straight line from 1F to 6Q.
Bridges	Where the road crosses a river.
Railway station	In square 4L
Church	With a steeple in square 8M.
Pub	In square 7H.
Wood	Covers 13Q, 13P, 13O, 12N and all the area to the east of these coordinates.
Post Office	In square 5H.
Village shop	In square 6I.

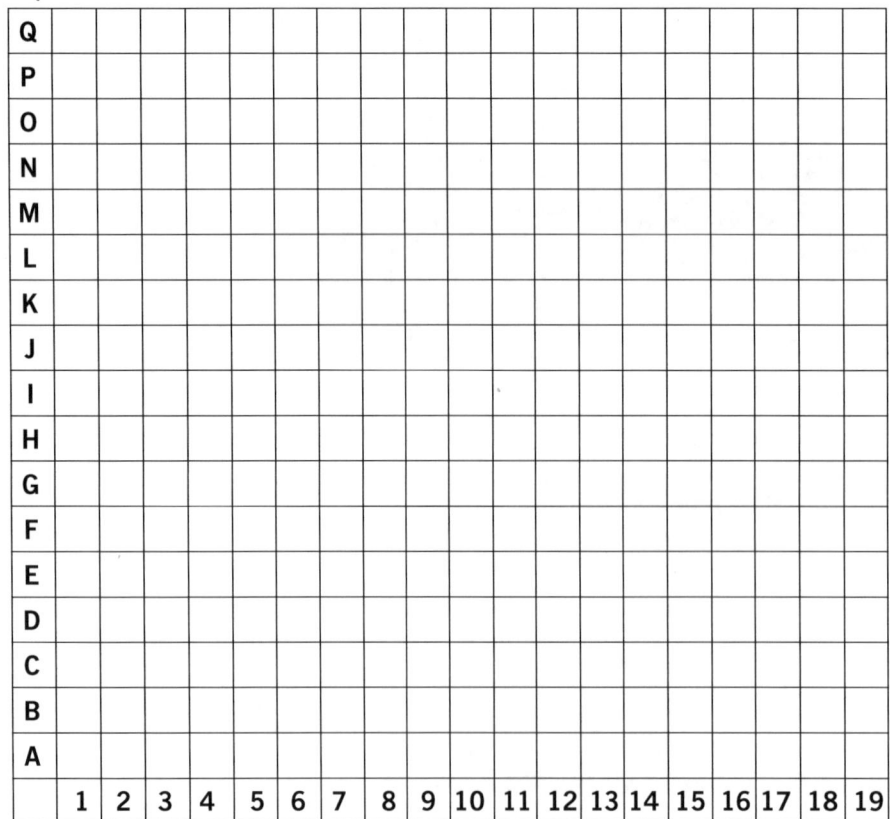

Key

 Add three more features to your sketch map and give the grid reference for each. Don't forget to design a symbol and add each to the key.

 What clues tell you Keysville is a fictional village?

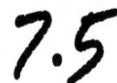

What are grid references?

Grid references can be used to help describe the location of a place on a map.

Imagine that you are stranded on a desert island and your only hope of rescue is to be spotted from the air!

You have made a grid on the beach in the sand like this.

G															
F															
E															
D															
C															
B															
A															
	1	**2**	**3**	**4**	**5**	**6**	**7**	**8**	**9**	**10**	**11**	**12**	**13**	**14**	**15**

❶ Carefully shade the squares using the key below. Tick each instruction as you do it. The pattern will begin to spell out a word that may save your life!

❷ Oh dear! The waves have washed away some of your letters! Guess what the word is and shade in the squares needed to complete it. Each time you shade a square, don't forget to write a grid reference for it in the table.

9B	11E	15B	1F	3D
15F	1E	1C	2D	5C
3C	13F	13D	11C	3E
15D	5F	8C	6F	12F
15E	5E	8E	6D	5D
13E	11D			

How do we use grid references?

Grid references can be used to help describe the location of a place on a map.

In this activity, you need to plan the design of a village.

Study the grid outline on Activity Sheet 7.6b. This shows the area in which your village will be designed.

- ◆ Draw two main **roads**. The roads must cross somewhere towards the centre of the grid.
- ◆ 90 squares should be used for **housing**.
- ◆ 50 squares should be used for **farmland**.
- ◆ 1 square should be used for a **farmhouse**.
- ◆ 18 squares should be used for **shops**, a **Post Office** and a **pub**.
- ◆ 1 square should be used for the **village pond**.
- ◆ 2 squares should be used for a **primary school** and **playground**.
- ◆ 4 squares should be used for a **sports field**.
- ◆ 2 squares should be used for a **doctor's surgery**.
- ◆ 4 squares should be used for **farm workers' cottages**.
- ◆ 10 squares should be used for a small **wood**.
- ◆ 1 square should be used for an **orchard**.
- ◆ 3 squares should be used for a **rural craft centre**.

1 Think about the types of symbols you will draw for each type of land use and complete the key below the map.

2 Start the map with the two main roads and then add other features to your map from the list above. Be careful! You will need to think carefully about where you will place each of the features.

3 Add further features to your village. Maybe a village green, a railway line, small roads, a new housing estate, a waste disposal and recycling centre, or even open space!

4 Be prepared to explain your village plan to your teacher. Give your village a name. Why did you plan the land use for your village the way you did?

How do we use grid references?

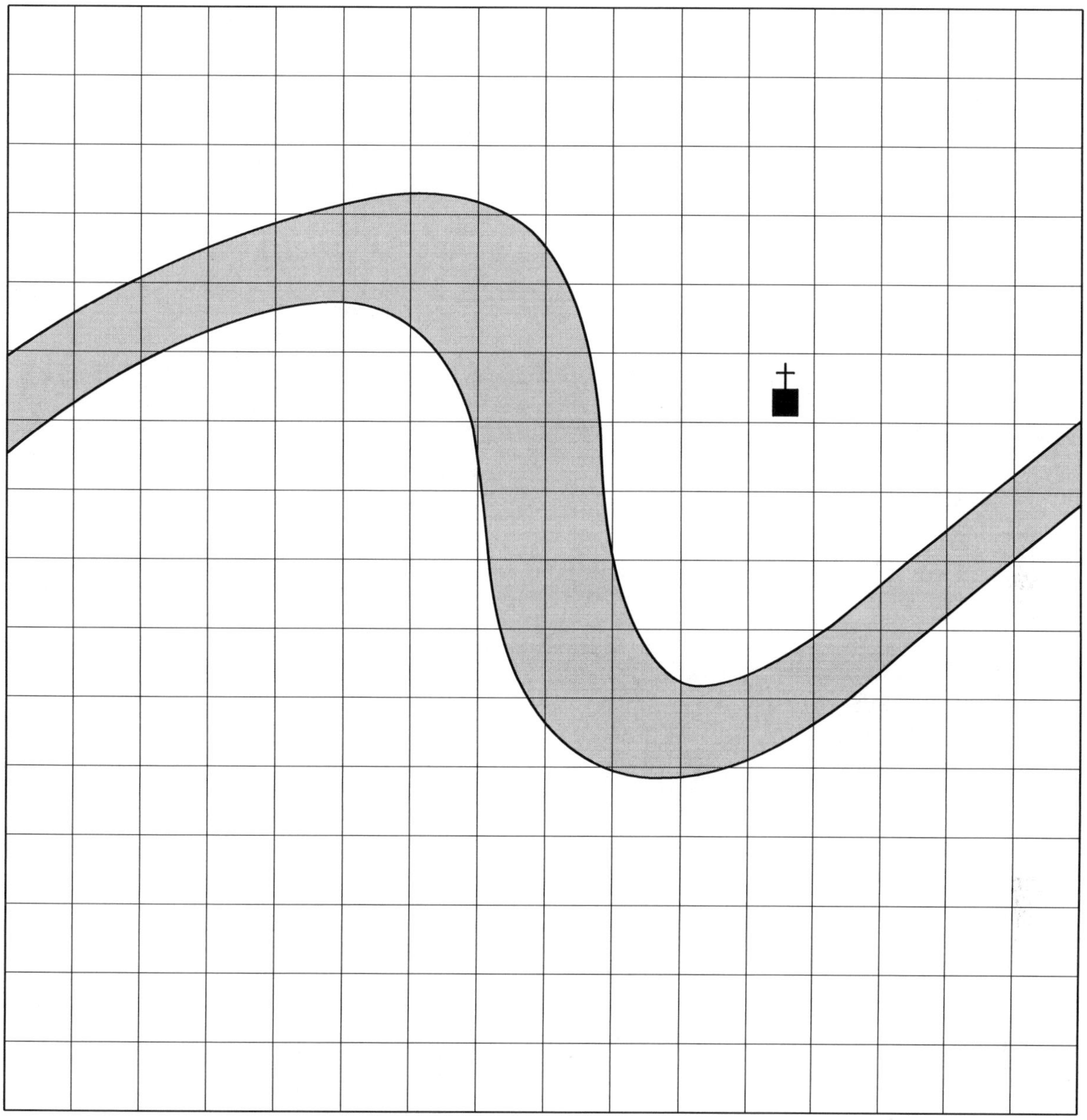

Key

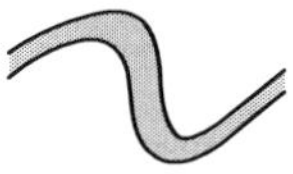

~~~~~~ River

♰
■ Church

How do we use six figure grid references?

Six figure grid references can be used to give the exact position of a place on a map.

◆ The **first three** numbers tell us how far to go along the bottom or top of the map. The third number tells us the number of tenths of a grid square.

◆ The **last three** numbers tell us how far to go up the sides of the map. The sixth number tells us the number of tenths of a grid square.

◆ On a map you will have to estimate the tenths of each grid square.

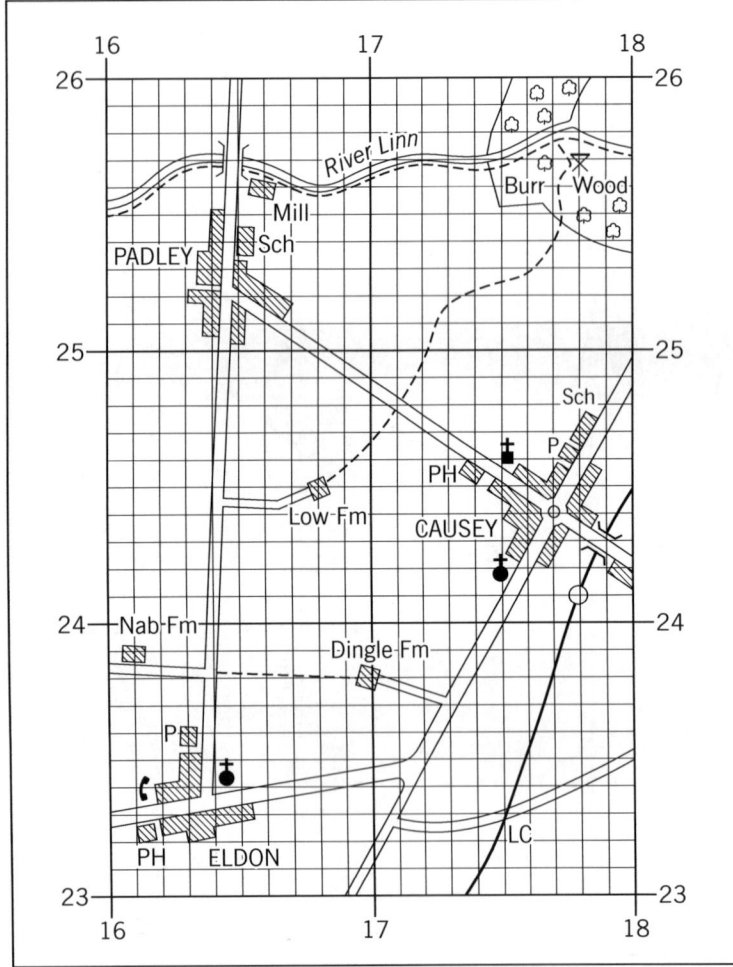

Sch	School		Church
P	Post Office		Telephone
PH	Public house		Picnic site
Fm	Farm		Bridge
LC	Level crossing		Railway station
	Woodland	- - -	Path

1   Add the following features to the map and key above using OS map symbols.

Camp site at 168243   Caravan site at 162242

Wind pump at 178237   Youth hostel at 174235

Orchard at 169241   Train station (closed to passengers) at 174231

2   Add three more features to the map and key.

◆ _____

◆ _____

◆ _____

How is height shown on a map?

Below is a relief map of the British Isles. The map
uses layer colouring to show height above sea level.

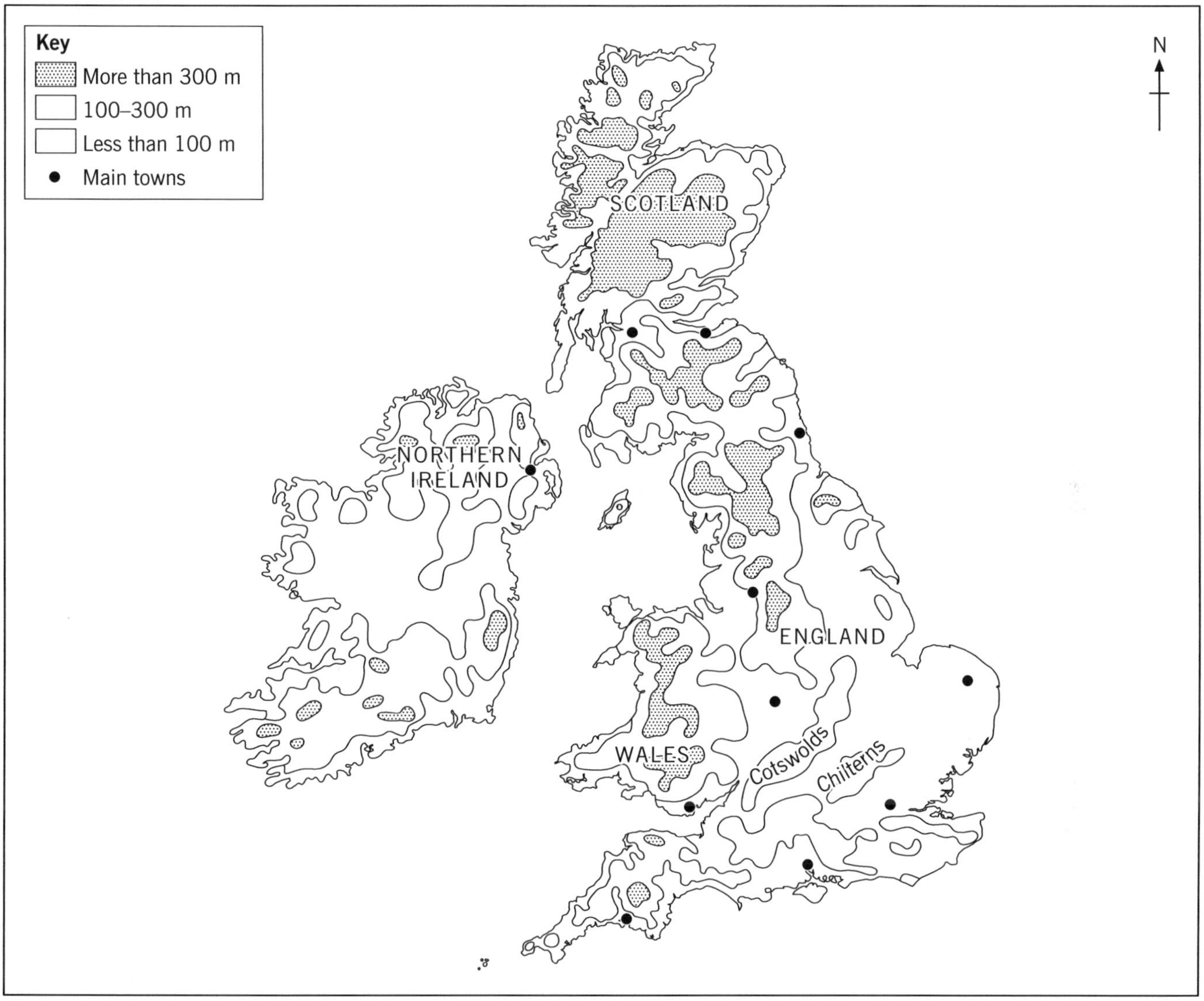

Key
- More than 300 m
- 100–300 m
- Less than 100 m
- ● Main towns

N

SCOTLAND

NORTHERN
IRELAND

ENGLAND

WALES   Cotswolds   Chilterns

 1   Show height on the map by layer colouring using coloured pencils.
- ◆ Colour areas more than 300 metres dark brown.
- ◆ Colour areas 100–300 metres light brown.
- ◆ Colour areas less than 100 metres green.
- ◆ Complete the key.

 2   Name the following highland areas on the map. Pages 133 and 137 in
the pupil book will help you.

     Cambrian Mountains   Lake District   Pennines

     Scafell Pike   Snowdon   Southern Uplands

 3   Name the following cities and towns on the map. Page 133 in the
pupil book will help you.

     Belfast   Birmingham   Cardiff   Edinburgh   Glasgow   London

     Manchester   Newcastle upon Tyne   Norwich   Plymouth   Southampton

How can height be shown on a map?

There are three main methods of showing height above sea level on maps.

◆ Spot heights are numbers that show the exact height of a place.

◆ Contours are lines on a map which join up places which have the same height.

◆ Layer colouring uses bands of different colours to show areas of different heights.

1 Complete the contour map below by following the instructions.

1 Finish joining the dots showing 10 to complete the 10 metre contour.	**2** Complete the 20 metre contour by joining the 20 dots.	**3** Complete the 30 metre contour by joining the 30 dots.	**4** Complete the 40 metre contour by joining the 40 dots.

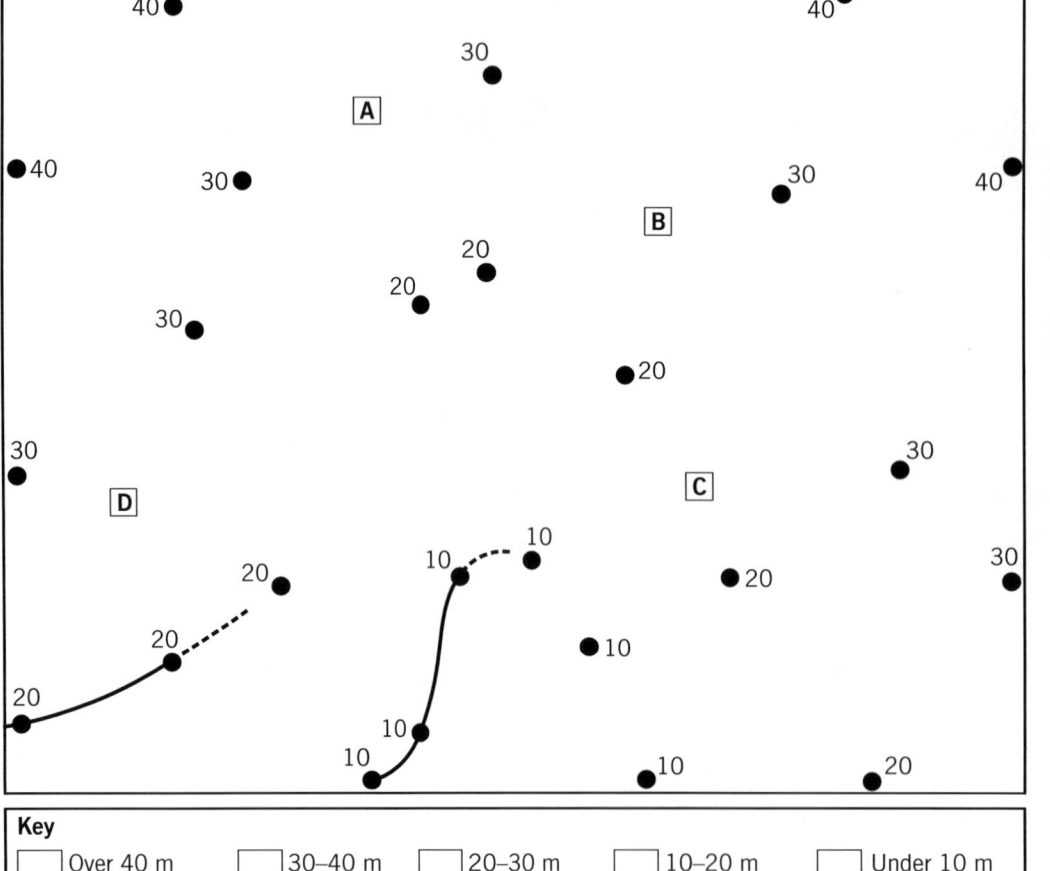

5 Colour land above 40 metres in brown.

6 Colour land between 30 and 40 metres in orange.

7 Colour land between 20 and 30 metres in yellow.

8 Colour land between 10 and 20 metres in light green.

9 Colour land under 10 metres in dark green.

10 Use coloured pencils to complete the key.

Key
☐ Over 40 m ☐ 30–40 m ☐ 20–30 m ☐ 10–20 m ☐ Under 10 m

2 Complete the following sentences:
◆ The height at A is _____ metres.
◆ The height at B is _____ metres.
◆ The height at C is _____ metres.
◆ The height at D is _____ metres.

3 Mark the place that you think has the lowest height with an 'X'.

How do contours show height and relief?

Contour lines are a good way of showing height and relief on a map.
Contours that are close together show steep slopes. Contours that are far
apart show gentle slopes. The pattern of the contours tells us about the
features of the land.

Match each of the landform sketches below to the correct contour
pattern by writing the correct letter in the space provided.

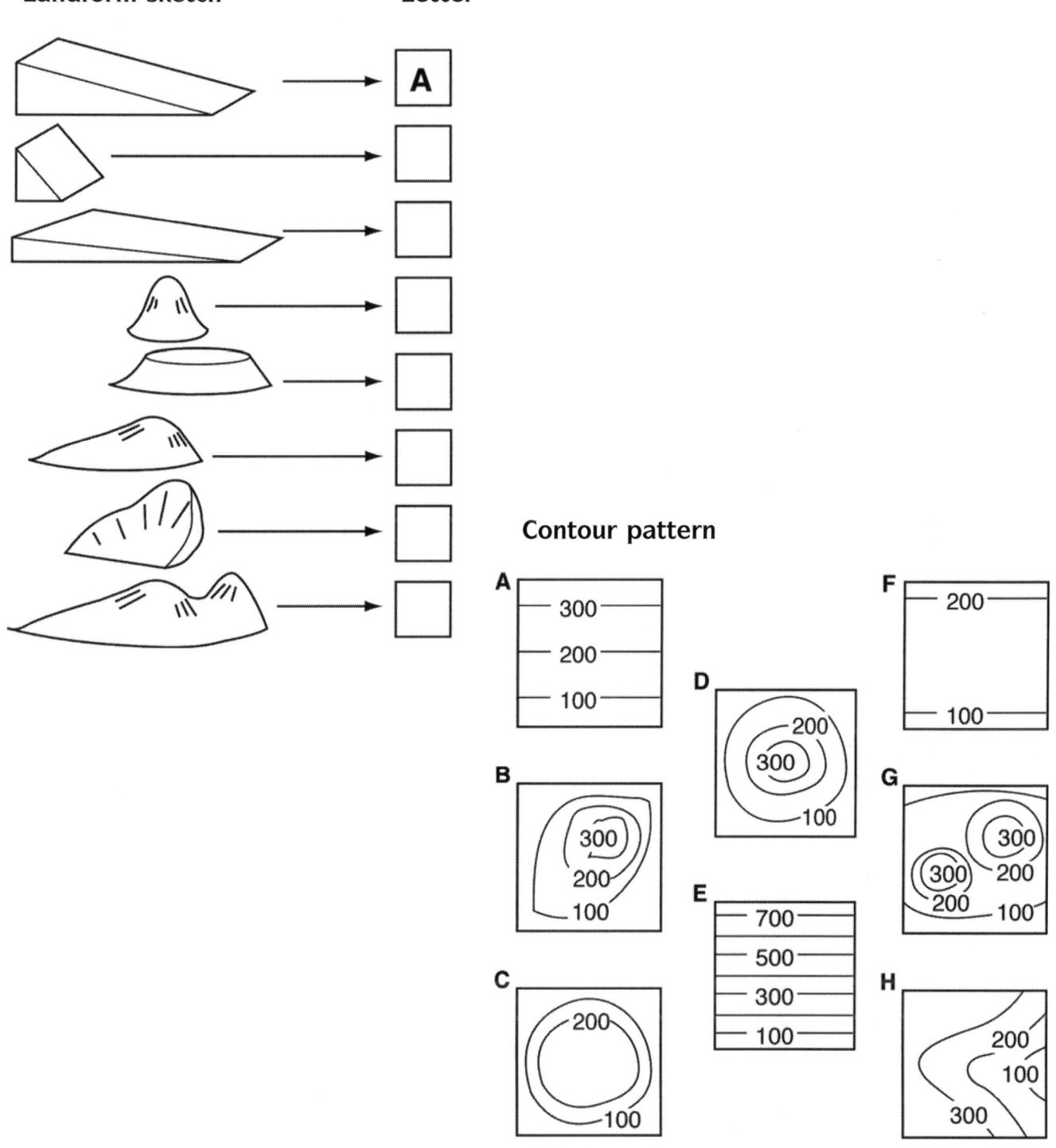

Landform sketch   **Letter**

Contour pattern

How can we describe routes?

Maps can be used to describe routes and places. Accuracy is very important when describing things.

A   Go to the *Key Geography Foundations* link on the Nelson Thornes website.

B   From the Map skills section, select the links to Multimap.

C   Enter the postcode of your home, and click 'Find'.
A street map will download, with the exact location of your home circled.

D   Select scale 1:50 000. An Ordnance Survey map of your neighbourhood will now download, again with your home circled.

E   Copy and paste this map into a word processing or desktop publishing program.

F   Use the software tools to describe and label places you know in your neighbourhood on the map.

G   Mark your route from your home to school (you may need to select a different scale of map).

H   Describe your route from your home to school. There is no need to try to include everything, but you must be very accurate. You might first describe the area in general and then mention both the physical features and human features. Write out the features in the order you would pass them.

I   Give six figure grid references to locate the main features observed on your journey.

As you finish each section of the map skills unit you should reflect on what you have learned. The table below will help you work out what you can do and what you might need some more practice with. (Page references refer to the pupil book.)

Task	My level of understanding	I must remember to...	Teacher assessment
Direction (pages126–127)	☺ ☺ ☹		☺ ☺ ☹
Distance (pages 128–129)	☺ ☺ ☹		☺ ☺ ☹
Map symbols (pages 130–131)	☺ ☺ ☹		☺ ☺ ☹
Four figure grid references (pages 132–133)	☺ ☺ ☹		☺ ☺ ☹
Six figure grid references (pages 134–135)	☺ ☺ ☹		☺ ☺ ☹
Height (pages 136–137)	☺ ☺ ☹		☺ ☺ ☹
Contours (pages 138–139)	☺ ☺ ☹		☺ ☺ ☹
Describing routes (pages 140–141)	☺ ☺ ☹		☺ ☺ ☹

Think about your learning!

Before you submit your final enquiry, spend some time thinking about the learning that you have carried out.

1 Look carefully at this list of skills. Geographers are skilled people! **Tick** the skills you are developing during your time working on this enquiry.

2 Describe **one** thing that enabled you to be successful in this task:

_____
_____
_____
_____
_____

3 Describe **one** problem you had, or thought you had, that stopped you from achieving your potential:

_____
_____
_____
_____
_____

Teamwork	☐
Reading	☐
Listening	☐
Discussion	☐
Problem solving	☐
Decision making	☐
Map interpretation	☐
Graphing	☐
Data analysis	☐
Questioning	☐
Debating	☐
Time management	☐
Presenting	☐
Empathy	☐
Annotation	☐
Evaluation	☐
Research	☐
Using ICT	☐
Comparing	☐

4 In these boxes write **two** actions that you will carry out to help you be more successful and reach your target in the future.